Charles-

Congrats on all your at Saybrus Partners!

I hope you enjoy this copy of "Walk off Winning."

All the best-

Stu Tp

"*Through his experience in college athletics, combined with his relation-ships with leaders in the business world, Steve identifies and describes the values that one must possess to build a strong culture. I also love his optimistic approach reinforcing the benefits of positive leadership. This book will benefit anyone who has a passion to become a better leader at work and in life!*"

— Jon Gordon, best-selling author of
The Energy Bus and *The Carpenter*

"*A one-of-a-kind leadership book.* Walk Off Winning *is a home run for leaders in all disciplines who are serious about creating and sustaining a championship team culture.*"

Chief Jason D. Umberger,
DeLand Police Department, FL

"*Coach Trimper is a walking, talking example of leadership – and now he's put his personality on paper with awesome real-life examples. You will feel his passion, energy, character, and motivation in* Walk off Winning, A Game Plan for Leading Your Team and Organization to Success *– all must-have traits for leadership and building strong cultures – on and off the field.*"

John Reed
president and CEO
Maine Savings FCU

"*We have had the privilege of working with Steve Trimper and have witnessed his ability to translate his superior coaching skills to leader-ship training in a business organization. Many similar correlations exist between successful team performance on the baseball field and your teams' successful performance in the business setting. In* Walk Off Winning, *Steve takes 19 core values essential in the development of a strong cul-ture and leadership ability, then uses them in easy-to-apply lessons for you and your organization. The book is packed with valuable insights for improving how you, as an individual, influence and impact your team as a coach and a leader."*

Carrie Darling Meo
vice president of Fixed Operations Darling's Auto Group
Jay Darling
president
Darling's Auto Group

"We were fortunate enough to have Steve Trimper present a leadership session at University Credit Union during our company wide training in the spring of 2015. While we knew that Steve would do a remarkable job with his presentation, we were not disappointed on that front nor with the impressive results we immediately noticed with our employees after the session. Steve inspired many in our workforce and he left a lasting impression of leadership with them which is still exhibited and referred to from time to time, almost two years after. He set the bar high for future trainers when he came to spend time with us and we feel fortunate to have gone through one of his coaching sessions."

Matthew J. Walsh
CPA president / CEO University Credit Union
Orono, Maine

"I had a very good employee of 17 year ask to meet with me this past week before she left her employment with CCI. In this meeting, she shared that a very traumatic event in her personal life several years ago, had, in her words, nearly paralyzed her from making major life decisions-that is until she heard you speak at our staff day when she was inspired to make a major career decision.

My staff appreciated your presentation and your talk was a key cog in a very successful staff gathering. Thanks again for your willingness to join us in Bethel."

C. Shawn Yardley
chief executive officer
Community Concepts
Lewiston, Maine

WALK OFF WINNING

STEVE TRIMPER

WALK OFF WINNING

A GAME PLAN FOR **LEADING YOUR TEAM** AND **ORGANIZATION** TO **SUCCESS**

WILEY

Published by John Wiley & Sons, Inc., Hoboken, New Jersey.

Published simultaneously in Canada.

For general information on our other products and services or for technical support, please contact our Customer Care Department within the United States at (800) 762-2974, outside the United States at (317) 572-3993 or fax (317) 572-4002.

Wiley publishes in a variety of print and electronic formats and by print-on-demand. Some material included with standard print versions of this book may not be included in e-books or in print-on-demand. If this book refers to media such as a CD or DVD that is not included in the version you purchased, you may download this material at http://booksupport.wiley.com. For more information about Wiley products, visit www.wiley.com.

Library of Congress Cataloging-in-Publication Data:
Names: Trimper, Steve, 1970- author.
Title: Walk off winning : a game plan for leading your team and
   organization to success / Steve Trimper.
Description: Hoboken, New Jersey : John Wiley & Sons, Inc., [2020] |
   Includes index.
Identifiers: LCCN 2019045135 (print) | LCCN 2019045136 (ebook) | ISBN
   9781119652205 (hardback) | ISBN 9781119652984 (adobe pdf) | ISBN
   9781119653011 (epub)
Subjects: LCSH: Leadership. | Teams in the workplace—Management. | Success
   in business.
Classification: LCC HD57.7 .T747 2020 (print) | LCC HD57.7 (ebook) | DDC
   658.4/092—dc23
LC record available at https://lccn.loc.gov/2019045135
LC ebook record available at https://lccn.loc.gov/2019045136

Cover image: © wuttichok /Getty Images
Cover design: Wiley

Printed in the United States of America

V10015964_120419

To Lisa, my wife, and daughters Ally and Morgan.
Love you guys.

Contents

Foreword

Ben Franklin recognized hard work, integrity, and persistence as essential to success, and these values resonated with my father and his children. They became the bedrock of our family business, which has always borne Franklin's name as tribute.

"Industry, perseverance, and frugality make fortune yield," said Franklin; and indeed, without a firm commitment to these three virtues, my father's fledgling mutual fund management company would not have grown into Franklin Templeton Investments, a global firm with more than $650 billion of assets under management. During my years at the firm's helm, we weathered dizzying ups and devastating downs in the market and unavoidable problems both natural and man-made, but as Franklin noted. "Those things that hurt, instruct.... Energy and persistence conquer all things."

Resilience is at the heart of any inventor, so it's no wonder Franklin was a model of perseverance. One cannot hope to harness electricity without suffering a few shocks! In any bold endeavor, the difference between success and failure is the extent to which one learns, adjusts, and keeps trying.

Franklin's core values are abundantly applicable in athletics, which may explain my affinity for sports. Growing up in Montclair, New Jersey, I played football, and as a young parent,

I enjoyed watching my sons play hockey and my daughter play soccer. I even coached her team for a time!

For as long as I can remember, I've been a baseball fan. In 1954, I was lucky enough to attend the World Series game where Willie Mays made an astonishing, on-the-run, over-the-shoulder catch to block Vic Wertz's deep center drive, contributing to a series sweep for the New York Giants. Enthusiastic journalists have tried to connect the dots between my early fandom and eventual purchase of an ownership stake in the San Francisco Giants, but honestly, I hadn't been pining for the team when the opportunity presented itself! Nonetheless, I appreciate the personal connection to a game that illustrates the value of working hard, playing by the rules, and never quitting.

In recent years, having moved from the San Francisco Bay Area to Palm Beach, Florida, I have had the pleasure of watching the development of the Division I baseball program at nearby Stetson University, where my grandson Charlie Bartlett majored in sports business and often joined me for ballgames or baseball talk. In 2018, as Charlie's graduation approached, our excitement revolved more around the diamond than his anticipated diploma, as the Hatters made an unprecedented run for the College World Series. Though ultimately thwarted, they earned a place among the top ten teams in the country and delivered the best performance in Stetson's history of intercollegiate baseball, dating back to 1901!

The team's success is certainly a credit to the players' exceptional talent, but talent alone is rarely sufficient. A winning record – in sports, business, and personal pursuits – reflects strong leadership, so I was curious about the Hatters' head coach, Steve Trimper, whom Stetson hired during Charlie's junior year, just weeks before the start of the season. A former player who began his Division I coaching career at Manhattan College, Steve had led the University of Maine's program since

2006, earning three conference titles and two trips to the NCAA Tournament, before arriving in DeLand. His bio confirmed the baseline credentials, but in getting to know Steve, I came to appreciate what he might call his "secret sauce," and the recipe was familiar.

Whether knowingly or not, Steve has honed his leadership as my family and I have, by adhering to the basic principles Ben Franklin espoused in his *Autobiography*. Surely, Steve knows the fundamentals of his particular business – the raw skills needed at the Division I level, the most effective ways to develop players' physical prowess, and the tactics most likely to yield the desired results over nine innings – but more importantly, he knows:

Values matter. Identifying and uniting around a few simple core values is essential for any organization to flourish. Circumstances will change but values are like the North Star. They'll keep you properly oriented and focused on your ultimate destination.

Baseball is a team sport and so is most everything else. Willie Mays made that extraordinary catch in the first game of the 1954 World Series, and the whole Giants team won, not just Mays. Even the most gifted individual can't go it alone. To succeed, surround yourself with good people and devote the time and energy necessary to build trust and develop loyalty.

There is no substitute for hard work. In Ron Shelton's 1988 film *Bull Durham*, Minor League Baseball veteran Crash Davis shares some wisdom with rookie phenom Nuke LaLoosh: "Sometimes you win. Sometimes you lose. Sometimes, it rains." At the University of Maine's flagship campus, sometimes it snows, and when faced with a blanketed field, Steve gathered his players and together they shoveled. A less diligent, less frugal response might have involved expensive equipment, excuses, or other bodies, but often we hold in our own hands the power to effect change and it's simply a matter of exercising that power – of doing it. Indeed, energy and persistence conquer all things.

Steve is a doer who has slowed down just long enough to capture in these pages the valuable lessons he's learned over the course of his unusual career. With characteristic, infectious exuberance, he offers a simple guide for developing leaders – and that's all of us, for as Franklin warned, "When you are finished changing, you're finished."

While Stetson baseball's recent success has generated lots of enthusiasm for the game locally, I'm occasionally troubled by indicators that America's pastime is falling out of favor with younger generations, too busy or too impatient for nine unpredictable innings of play. The beauty of the game is unfortunately lost on some, but I continue to delight in the intricate maneuvering and deliberate pacing, in the knowledge that it ain't over till it's over.

Baseball, like life, is a long game by design. Cultivate a strong team, prepare as best you can, give it your all, and work to improve a little bit every day. Keep swinging. And walk off winning.

Charles Johnson
principle owner of the San Francisco Giants MLB team
retired chairman and CEO of
Franklin Templeton Investments

Introduction

eadership and _success_ are two words that seem to be exploited on a daily basis in places like the boardroom and the locker room. Supervisors and coaches alike engage in a multitude of practices to have members of their team transform into what they believe are better leaders in order to help steer their organization to greatness. They say powerful words like _culture, values, traits,_ and _cohesiveness,_ yet are they able to accomplish these things?

In today's competitive workplace environment, where production goals and targets need to be met, supervisors are looking for that secret sauce to give their organization an edge over others. The same thing exists on the playing fields. More and more, coaches are taking away valuable practice time on the field and spending it in the classroom preaching values, culture, and leadership.

With so many ideas, books, speakers, and theories on the topic of leadership floating around the corporate and sports worlds, how do you decipher what's best for your unit? You wonder, "How am I gonna get our team to gel? Work harder? Beat our competition?" "Who or what is available to help me accomplish this?" These days, just grab a snack from any airport newsstand and you'll see a tree of leadership books staring you in the face!

So, what problem drives you to seek out all this information? It could be that you aspire to build a better corporate or athletic team. Maybe you need to improve morale or create a better culture in your office. You may even recognize the problem that needs to be addressed, but don't have a clue how to do this.

You've already taken the first step toward improvement; that is, you are certainly motivated to search for information to improve your teams' culture. Heck, it's probably why you chose this leadership book to add to the growing shelf of literature behind your desk.

You're no different than I am – on a daily basis I absorb any success story or leadership trait I deem worthy. I strive to increase my ability to lead. You and I want to be lifelong learners, motivated to bring the best out in those around us.

Less Inside Baseball, More Inside Leadership

As we navigate this book, we are going to discuss ideas that will help you on your way to leadership success. Each chapter is designed to give you a set of values that I have not only observed from other great leaders, but that have helped me when implementing quality leadership into businesses, teams, or organizations. Ultimately, these values will lead to a strong culture within your organization, able to withstand the ebbs and flows that come with any organization over time.

Think of each chapter as an important value or trait that is essential to practice. Your goal is to implement these into your leadership portfolio in order to build and sustain a strong culture within your work or team environment. Whether you strive to make your team more cohesive, establish core values, or improve culture, this book will help you to accomplish this.

All too often people just *talk* about doing these things. Someone I call the "Sayer" is one who talks a big game, announcing how they will change the culture or implement a leadership plan, never to follow through. But you will walk away from this book with a plan to *do* them! You will ultimately become a "Doer," someone who addresses issues head on, knowing there will be both success and failure. You won't be intimidated or fearful of change and will become addicted to the challenges and celebrations that true leadership can provide you on a daily basis.

Through a multitude of stories and experiences I have been fortunate to have lived or heard, I will share important and proven values that have led some of the greatest people that touched my own career to long-term success. Each story represents a value that these individuals learned to invest in to be great leaders when building a strong organizational culture. Though many failures and setbacks, they all rose to the top by following a positive path.

You might be surprised that most of the lessons I have learned have little or no relation to baseball or even to sports in general. They are derived from small and large business owners and leaders who failed time and time again, only to grind away for long hours to build their empire. They might be administrators who didn't have a ton of financial support or resources, yet still made the most of their situation.

Of course, my job is to tell these stories and messages in a way that piques your interest and helps you gain ideas to implement the strategies in your career, with your team, and in everyday life with your friends and family. When you finish, you will improve as a leader and be a motivating influence in both your professional and your personal life. You will improve at the sometimes difficult task of finding the right people to join your organization, and will have a positive impact on those around you. You'll experience that feeling of success or big advancement at your job—that same feeling you get with a *walk-off win*!

For those of you who aren't diehard baseball fans, I'll explain the concept of a walk-off win. Imagine that it's the bottom of the ninth, the score is tied, and your team is up to bat. It's crunch time! There are two out with a runner on second base. As you, the batter, dig into the batter's box to face the imposing, hard-throwing closer (pitcher) on the mound, you recognize the count is three balls and two strikes. The next pitch thrown to you will make you the hero or the goat. As that 90-mile-an-hour fastball heads your way, things go into slow motion. You are so focused and locked in, you actually see the tiny red laces on the ball.

As you make the split-second decision to launch the bat from your shoulder, you feel the bat connect with the ball and hear the sweet *crack* when it happens. The ball finds the outfield for a hit and the runner is chugging around third base, trying to score that winning run.

As the player in the field picks up the ball and throws it to the catcher in an attempt to tag that runner out, the runner slides into home plate. You run to first base after your hit, but your focus is on the play at the plate the whole time. As the dust settles and the umpire signals "Safe," your teammates rush from the dugout and tackle you in celebration of your hit, and the walk-off win!

So keep reading, and you too will get a walk-off win. Your leadership skills will grow, resulting in success in the boardroom, the class room, on the playing field, and in your everyday life.

Learning from Coaches, Mentors, and Other Great Leaders

Being in the field of college athletics for over 27 years has certainly taught me a lot about sports. The parents out there might be able to appreciate the fact that my day revolves around

35 young adults, ages 18–22. Although my hair is still atop my head, it changed to a shade of salt and pepper many years ago.

But what has been my blessing has been the multitude of people who taught me not about baseball but about leadership. It took me some time to figure this out, but when I did, I was able to become a better mentor to the individuals who surrounded me.

More than 11 years ago, a local financial institution asked me to give a presentation on my thoughts of what makes a quality leader and builds a strong team. Since that day, my ideas on quality leadership have grown and evolved, along with a set of successful core values to instill in those who entrusted me to help them.

Time and time again, when I finished a presentation to a group, people would ask me where they could find my book to further research my discussion. Book? You're crazy. Maybe someday, I would say. Give me a flash drive and I can download my PowerPoint presentation for you. That's all I had.

Well, it's finally time for me to stop saying I was gonna write that book "someday." I am shifting from being a "Sayer" to a "Doer." I'm ready to work outside my comfort zone of baseball and become an author. As you read about the power of giving, along with the importance of serving others, you'll learn my thoughts about implementing successful leadership strategies and strong culture into your own organization or team.

So, I hope you can sit back and enjoy many of the stories that led me to believe in the importance of investing in core values and building a strong culture within your organization. Leading the people around you through both the good times as well as all the muck that can come with failure will ultimately enable you to reach true success.

1

You Need Values, But Keep Them Simple

When it comes to the hot topics in today's world of leadership, there is much confusion about the path you must navigate as you embark on improving as a leader. The market is saturated with leadership books, and certainly many have great value. Yet many of the theories and ideas tend to mimic one another.

However, I find myself a bit confused when I research the components it takes to be a great leader. The jumble of words and subtopics can be intimating and overwhelming. Here is where I believe many go down the wrong path, either trying to be someone they are not, or attempting to implement too many ideas. I always preach to be great at one thing instead of being good at many. It allows you to stand out among your peers.

1

The Flowchart of True Success

I want to take a moment to talk about a sort of flowchart that can better describe a path to being a successful leader. I like using flowcharts because they summarize the decisions and movement of information, giving us a clear and concise path from beginning to end to solve an issue or problem. And although leadership should not be considered an issue or problem, it certainly has steps to follow as you work to lead your group and organization to true success. You can always revert back to each step as you set new goals, but the steps tend to happen in the order shown in Figure 1.1.

Leadership, in my mind, begins with traits. Traits can be a characteristic quality that distinguishes certain features of that person. They are practices you engage in and help you build a foundation of personal tendencies and have a hand in defining your personality. Some common examples are honesty, integrity, work ethic, and character.

The next phase of leadership concerns values. Values are thoughts, beliefs, and attitudes that you and your group have invested in emotionally. Although they too can aid in defining your personality, don't confuse values with traits. Traits help

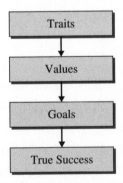

FIGURE 1.1 The steps of leadership.

us establish our set of values. Values also have importance in building an organization's culture; they are shared among the group and are practiced over time in order to reach successful goals.

Once our values are present, it gives us goals to work toward daily. Goals are measurable benchmarks that are established for you and your group to reach a level of success. It could be an increased number of accounts a business might add over a six-month period of time, leading to better results for that particular business. Or it could be a certain time you set for yourself in a 5K road race. Goals provide a sort of finish line so you can feel a sense of accomplishment when they're reached.

And when goals are met, this rewards us with a sense of true success. Success is the reward for your group when they achieve positive results over sustained periods of time. The difference between goals and success is that goals are one-time tests we set for ourselves to achieve. Success is when we reach multiple goals time and time again to build prosperity for an organization over the long term.

So, let's think about our flowchart, starting with traits. Traits drive us to succeed through the strong values we cherish. If we are dedicated and determined to work at being great at these values, they will help us reach any goals we set for our organization. Reaching these goals will have rewards, leading to the long-term success of our organization.

Be Selective When Establishing Values

As you navigate your quest to improve as a leader, be careful not to bite off more than you can chew. There are so many quality values, it is very difficult to tackle a broad range of them. Let me give you an example.

In my current role as a Division I college baseball coach, I obviously need to have good student athletes who are willing to work hard each day to improve individually, both in the classroom and on the playing field. However, as in any business or organization, the culture we establish is vital to our success. In most businesses, when you introduce a set of values, everyone is excited to dive in and work to achieve the culture you, as a leader, strive to create.

But as time moves forward, many veer off this path. This is due to a few reasons. First, the leader who is preaching the values and culture may be inexperienced, and may have a difficult time consistently bringing the entire group back on track. They might talk a good game about leadership but not follow through on their ideals and demands. This usually leads to trust issues and second-guessing by the team, making it nearly impossible to establish a strong and lasting culture within the organization. In the following chapters, I will share a few stories, both fictitious and genuine, that demonstrate how difficult it is to be consistent as a leader.

Another reason may be that the group is confused or overwhelmed by the plethora of information given to everyone. Supervisors bring in guest speakers to energize the organization. They purchase books like the one you are currently entranced by, only to fail to follow up in working constantly on culture every waking moment. Webinars are purchased and viewed. All this information can flood the group with information overload.

> All this information can flood the group
> with too much substance.

Returning from a recent speaking engagement on leadership, I found myself at one of those airport convenience stores at the Atlanta airport. Right there next to the checkout counter, among the bottles of water and packs of gum, was a tree of books, above which was a sign reading, "The Leadership Business Center." There must have been 30 books about leadership. Certainly, many of them are quite good, and in fact I make it a habit to pick some up to see if I can learn a bit. But it illustrates my point about the amount of information available to us: it's both a great thing and an overwhelming occurrence.

Improve What You Already Have

When I first arrived at Stetson as the baseball coach, our athletic director, Jeff Altier, wanted to do whatever he could to help the program jump forward and compete on the national stage. Being a small, private university of around 3,000 students can be challenging when competing against larger schools such as the University of Florida, Florida State, Mississippi State, or the University of North Carolina.

Those universities have huge financial support for many of their programs, in both athletics and academics. So, Jeff embarked on a mission, not to compete with these teams in terms of finances, but to improve our situation at Stetson, in any way he was capable of. His message to me? Focus on improving what you have, not what you can't get.

That doesn't mean Jeff won't shoot for the stars, and give a great effort. But we were not capable of building an $85 million stadium like a certain Division I program near our university. We just simply did not have the resources. So he and our director of development worked to raise the funds to renovate our locker room and players' lounge area. We both agreed this would lend us a recruiting edge, because players like to have nice things.

> You haven't achieved success just because
> you drive a shiny car.

However, you haven't achieved success just because you drive a shiny car. That locker room, or stadium, or fancy corner office with the nice leather chair, is a fishing lure. It is meant to attract talent. Catch one's eye. Once you have them attracted, well, then the hard work starts for the supervisor. This is where you build your culture.

Jeff and Mike McKercher, our director of athletic development, went on to raise over $500K, which lead to a *huge* improvement in our situation. Not only did we receive a brand-new shiny locker room, with a Stetson-logoed Ping-Pong table to boot, but we established a players' lounge from a large wasted closet area. This room was designed to fit about 30 people comfortably, and allowed our players to have a spot to relax, with a few TVs, two desks for studying, and a full kitchen, where snacks and hydration stations were installed.

As the project was nearing completion, I saw a great opportunity to visually establish our culture. Like many locker rooms, office areas, and places of business, people add quotes, phrases, words of importance, and other sayings in highly visible areas to remind everyone of their idea of a great culture. Our players' lounge had a long wall painted green to show off the school colors. But I envisioned this great space as our "values wall."

As Jeff, my boss, would attest, I have a knack for adding to these projects well after they begin. I am really good at spending money after a clear and concise budget, along with the scope of work, has been established. So one day I spoke to Jeff's assistant, Stacy, and bribed her with a bit of kindness to get on his schedule—unannounced, of course.

"Jeff, I got this great idea—ya gotta let me try this. *It will be awesome!* I want to add a wall wrap of pictures and words to establish our team culture! It will be *great!* And it's only gonna cost..."

In classic Jeff style, he didn't say no. He saw my enthusiasm and agreed to find a way. So, I set out with my team to get the values wall going.

Don't Make the Wall Too Big

I wanted to be clear to the players that they were embarking on an important project to establish our values that embody the culture of the Stetson Baseball Program. This was a long-term deal, with an impact far into the future.

Without telling the players what I was planning, I asked everyone to text me one word, saying, meaning, or phrase they thought would best define what we wanted our program to represent for many years to come. With 35 ball players on the roster, I knew I would get all kinds of replies: toughness, blue collar, win, culture, grit, work ethic, and many more.

I put every one of their responses on the wall wrap. Their words and phrases were blasted in huge bold letters on this wall, spanning over 40 feet, for everyone to see.

After it was installed, we had an unveiling party. They all funneled into the players' lounge, where I explained to the group, "This is where the work really starts. This wall of words and phrases was established by you, and will be part of this program for years to come."

Now, we all agreed that the 30-plus items on that wall were important, but I explained they were incapable of "doing" all these things. I saw the puzzled looks on their faces, as they thought I was questioning their ability to work. I went on to explain that was not the case. But the true test of their culture was going to be whittling down all of these items to a select few that we would work to be great at. The information overload presented by all these values would surely lead us to being just mediocre at them, rather than of being great at a small portion.

I left them in that room to figure out what was most important, and I made it abundantly clear that when they established the list, we were not going to *talk* about being great at these. We would *do* whatever it took to be great. So I cautioned them not to come back to me with an unrealistic number of values.

Well, after about an hour, they did exactly that. They had a list of about ten items. Here is where I had to hold my ground, as one of their leaders, and send them back to make the list more realistic.

After another few minutes, they returned with six. Nope, still too many.

I was hoping we could establish four. Four values we would talk about, work on, address when we had failures, and try to improve every day we walked though that locker room door.

They returned with those four: EXCELLENCE, COMMITMENT, CHARACTER, and INTEGRITY.

There we had it. Very powerful words.

I wanted them to understand the huge responsibility it would take to uphold the definitions of the words they chose. Trying to be great at 30, 20, even 10 of these would lead to overload. In that case we would only be talking those values, not living them every day.

Create Your Wall and Work on It Daily

Fast-forward two-plus years, and those words are engrained in our program. They not only appear on the values wall, but are blasted in the dugout and the locker room, and appear on sticky notes I leave daily in their personal space.

And it is not easy to enact these four values every day. It takes tremendous effort. Pieces of our program will inevitably change, including players, coaches, and support staff. New faces have to be schooled on these words and their importance to the future success of our program.

> That's when we have to be at our best, in those difficult times.

The words those players choose come with great responsibility to work at being great, even when we are going through the muck. When things are not going our way, when failure is present—that's when we have to be at our best, in those difficult times.

I challenge you, as a leader trying to improve the culture within your organization, to have your team create your own values wall. Explain to your people the importance of being great, one value at a time. Focus all your energy, time, and resources at this one value and it will eventually lead you to another.

As their leader, you can help them navigate through this process, reward them when the organization's culture strengthens, and guide them to the next step in the long-term success of your organization. We will tackle the "how to" as we move forward with the coming chapters.

Coach's Challenge

1. Define four important traits you want your organization to have.
2. Define four values you want your organization to have.
3. What is the most important trait or value already in place with your organization that you can improve upon?
4. What can you do, as a leader, to remind your people of your "wall" on a daily basis?

2

Never Underestimate the Power of Giving

I coach Division I baseball: my dream job. But along the way I have learned two very important lessons. Like most people, I had no clue about these lessons until years later.

Create a Foundation for Success

The first lesson happened when I was hired for my first head coaching job. The athletic director at Manhattan College, Bob Byrnes, treated me like a son. I was so pumped—28 years old and a DI coach! I had so much energy, I started the day I was hired.

He did what he could to help me be successful at a low-level coaching job—no home field, a small budget, one-third the scholarships allowed by NCAA rule, not even an indoor batting cage. But it was the right job for me. Of course, I wanted a stadium, a bigger budget, all the benefits the boys had at Miami, or Clemson. Each time I drove by the Yonkers raceway parking lots on my way to work, I would dream of finding a way to get a stadium built there. As far-fetched as it was, I always thought we could get something better. I wanted it all.

In order for Bob to attract a coach for a full-time position, he convinced the college president that the coach could also be a marketing director for all sports. This would, it was hoped, off-set the costs of the position and make some cash for the school. I had no real interest in being a marketing guy, but if selling a few advertisements in the gym helped me become Division I coach, so what?

When I first arrived, all I wanted to do was coach. I believed I needed good assistants, but I only had $4,000 for that. I asked Bob for a graduate position, and he agreed. Next, I wanted a batting cage. "Bob, we need this desperately." Bob agreed. Bob gave me what he could, and then some. He saw my effort, and felt the risk was worth the reward. It was a gamble—the president was watching closely too, and Bob would have some explaining to do if it didn't work. I was too inexperienced to fully understand it. I was in "want" mode.

Eventually, Bob had to explain that I was going to have to get off the baseball gig for a bit and find some donors and sponsors. I acted like a seven-year-old whose parents had just taken away his toys. I wanted nothing to do with that part of the job. I made excuses every day for weeks.

Bob had a great sense of humor, but you definitely knew when he was not happy with you. He called me in to his office one day. Bob was sitting in the big old rotating chair, with his back to his desk, and I was left with the wooden schoolboy chair in front of the desk. Bob can appear intimidating; he's a big man, a football guy in his college days. In fact, he coached football very successfully in New Jersey after he graduated from Manhattan College.

Without turning around to face me, Bob asked, "So, tell me, where we are with sponsors?"

The fast-talking, nervous me came out with all the excuses. "It's too tough, there's not enough time, I gotta get the team in order first." I even complained about the park where we practiced, saying that I spent extra time picking up glass so the guys sliding wouldn't cut themselves.

I was met with deafening silence, long enough to make me squirm. Was he mad? Did he even hear me?

He then did something I will never forget. He quietly opened a drawer and passed me a piece of paper over his shoulder. "Here, Steve. Just sign that at the bottom and we are all good."

One glance at the top of the document and my heart sank. Across the top I read: "My resignation letter."

"Steve, I don't want anything to do with making you unhappy. You clearly don't have what it takes and I misread you when I hired and gave you a chance. So, let's move on and not waste our valuable time."

I sat in frozen silence, realizing he was quite serious. When he finally spun around in his chair, I picked up my head and looked at him as squarely as I could.

Bob's eyes got red and he took a big deep breath. His nose scrunched a bit, and he spoke. It was my first real gift.

"Let me tell you something, son. I brought you here because I believed you could handle all that would be dealt to you. It's not gonna be easy. So you need to decide, right now, are you gonna be a guy who looks for what you don't have, or will you work with what you're given and try to fix it. Are you a person who only likes to work on things you like to do, or are you willing to tackle the things that aren't fun with the same vigor? Because, if you can't have this mentality, you cannot be part of my team."

> Focus on what you can control, and if
> you want to change it, then find a way.

Bob taught me a valuable lesson: focus on what you can control, and if you want to change it, then find a way. It's not always going to be easy, and it certainly won't happen without effort.

"Listen, son, I told most people that I made you the marketing director to raise money and justify the position. But the real reason I made marketing part of the position is that if you want to be a great coach, then you need to learn how to market and promote. Promote your program, promote yourself. Market everything you can, and it will open up great doors.

"I saw that in you. So learn the art of cultivating. Learn the art of relationship building. Master these, and only then will you know how many opportunities will be presented to you."

It hit me like a ton of bricks. "Yes, sir! Got it!"

Bob was using a marketing position to push me to be a great promoter because he knew that someday it would help make me a better college baseball coach. I hustled out of his office, clutching the resignation letter and tearing it to shreds as the door closed behind me.

Today, some two decades later, I owe Bob an awful lot. When I complained to him about what I didn't have, I had no idea how much fundraising, donor relations, cultivation, and relationship building I had on the horizon in my career as a coach. It clearly has been the one of the main reasons I have been successful.

Back then, I would have said that success is measured in the wins. But without Bob, there would have been very few wins.

There would have been no foundation, no pillars on which to build success—the true success of people, relationships, loyalty, and trust.

So the second, and most important, gift Bob gave me after awarding me the position was how to be something other than a baseball coach.

A Gift of Giving Might Be Right Under Your Nose

After my second season, one of the strangest yet life-changing meetings took place. I received a call from a raspy-voiced New Yorker twang by the name of John Mullen. A Manhattan alum who played in the late '80s, John was very blunt and to the point. He wanted to coach. He had no experience, other than playing for four years while at Manhattan College. I knew from reading past media guides that the 1980s teams weren't the most successful.

Initially, I was pretty skeptical that a 30-something guy, living in New York City and who had never coached, wanted to coach Division I baseball. He explained that he was not looking to be paid but would volunteer his services. After a short in-person meeting, we agreed that John would join us that coming fall. But I was fully expecting that I would need to hold his hand every step of the way and hope he didn't do anything to embarrass me.

Well, John was great. He didn't know much about coaching and teaching, but he had passion. He was always early and he stayed at the field until the last guy left. He listened. He asked questions. He was the calm of the team when I was going haywire over a disputed call with an umpire or yelling at a player for not hustling.

For two years, I could not figure out why he was putting in all this time for no money. I wondered how he made his living.

He did, after all, drive a very nice Mercedes to practice each day. But I knew from our long bus talks that the family wasn't rich. His dad was an insurance salesman. Must've sold a lot of insurance, I thought.

One day, while we were out to dinner during a weekend series in Albany, New York, John and I finally had a chat about his background. He explained that he had been following in his old man's footsteps, selling insurance in midtown Manhattan, working extremely hard for long hours, dealing with cold calls and rejections. He told me how he and his partner in the office worked on a huge case for a year, one that landed the company millions. On the night of closing the deal, they celebrated, expecting big promotions. But the next day they learned that all they would receive for their efforts was a gift card to a local restaurant.

John and his partner instantly made a life-changing decision. We can do this ourselves, they thought. With no money and no clients, they set out to start their own home healthcare business. Ten years later, despite failures, setbacks, and many learning experiences, John and his partner had built a multimillion-dollar home healthcare business, with over 300 employees.

I was in shock. Now I knew why he always tried to pick up the dinner tab when we are on the road. I asked him why it took two years for us to have this conversation.

It was quite simple, he explained. First, he didn't want us to be co-workers or friends based on his success and money. Far too often, when people knew of his success, he felt the relationship was not genuine. Second, he wanted to give back to the school. Although Manhattan College baseball was far from successful in terms of wins during John's playing days, he learned important values that he attributed to his success as he built his company. So, he simply wanted to give a gift and be a part of the next generation of Manhattan College baseball.

Giving Leads to Loyalty

There is more to the giving that both Bob and John did for me. Remember, these two individuals were highly successful in their field of work, and were more advanced as leaders than I was at this stage of my career. The biggest by-product of their generosity was unwavering loyalty.

From the lessons they both taught me when I was in the beginning stages of my career, coupled with the gift of giving they provided, I became extremely loyal to both of them. My focus was to prove to them I was worth the effort and energy they invested in me. I didn't want to ever let them down.

Because they both were so supportive of my career and really showed me they wanted to help me be successful, I found myself working harder, putting in longer days recruiting, and—as Bob taught me—focusing on the things I had, not what I lacked. I gave great effort at my job and wanted to impress them. They were both invested in me, so I felt a responsibility to prove my value to them.

The formation of loyalty within an organization, or that bond between two individuals, is a huge factor in long-term success. In later chapters, I will circle back to loyalty and how it effects the outcome of a business, organization, or a team.

> Invest in people, and those people will be
> great producers for you in the future.

And that right there—the giving of lifelong lessons, support, love, and even a kick in the fanny to motivate—is the gift of giving. Bob and John were way over my pay grade at this stage of my career when it comes to being a leader. They taught me that when you truly invest in someone, giving up your own time, energy, and even sometimes money, the life lessons that are received can be the greatest gift. They both were masters at this. Invest in people, and those people will be great producers for you in the future.

No wonder they continued to be successful. Bob went on to be a Hall of Fame member in multiple athletic administrator organizations and retired as one of the most respected members not only in the Manhattan College community, but in the field of NCAA Division I athletics.

John has that magic touch. He is somewhat of a calculated risk taker, which is what makes him so successful. Since his days of volunteering with me in the early 2000s, he has since sold Trinity Health Care for a crazy number, invested in a horror film that netted him over $10 million, bought three successful restaurants on Long Island, owns a few car washes, and is even heavily invested in the app business – all things outside his comfort zone.

Yet, despite their great success, they never lost the power to give, and more important, to invest in people.

> When you give back, you will eventually
> get something in return.

To this day, John and Bob have been two of my closest friends, and their gifts came in bunches. They were two of the first people I interviewed when I set out to be a better coach and try to understand the definition of success. They explained that when you give back, you will eventually get something in return, and it doesn't always have to be money. They gave back to Manhattan baseball or gave me resources to be successful in the early stages of my career as a baseball coach. They received a lifelong friend, my knowledge in the sport, and what they could take from our baseball team's success and turn into their own personal success.

In a way, John and Bob were cutting edge, ahead of their time. In 1999, there were not a lot of books about building successful businesses in relation to sport teams. Yet they saw the value of giving to me, aiding in the success of the Manhattan College baseball program, and therefore producing the by-product of me working hard to prove to them I deserved their support.

As you navigate through your own work environment, be on the lookout for times when you can give. Identify co-workers who need a pep talk or mentoring; this seemingly small gesture can lead to the gift of reciprocity. Your gift of giving within your office with an employee or supervisor can give back to you in a larger sense. You could receive important values from others, such as loyalty, trust, dedication, commitment, and so on.

So John and Bob both taught me that giving to someone will eventually lead to receiving valuable information and experiences, but only if you are looking for those values, and it took me years to truly understand the gifts I was given. The more you give, the more you get in return.

Coach's Challenge

1. Identity a challenge at your workplace over which you have control. Can you find a way to influence change for the better?

2. Name an instance where you gave someone at your office something of value and where you were able to get something in return. Your gift might have been advice, a book, or even your time.

(*Continued*)

3. Find one person in whom to invest your time and mentoring and watch their growth within your company and as a producer for the business.

4. Who has given you a gift to help you grow in both everyday life and at the workplace?

5. What can you identify that you gave someone who helped you?

3

Attitude and the Power of the Handshake

Have you ever been in such a great mood that everything feels as perfect as it can get? It could be for many different reasons; maybe your boss gave you a great recommendation, or your kids are doing well in school. This frame of mind allows you to sleep well at night, and gives you a bounce in your step in the morning. Weekdays and weekends blend together, with no Monday morning blues or Wednesday hump day tempers, as you cherish every day and attack it with energy and vigor.

I hope you've had the chance to experience this state of mind at some point. Most of us dream of hovering in this constant state of happiness all the time. But likely, that is not the case.

Most people allow a multitude of situations to influence them throughout the day.

Case in point: You had a great week at work. The project you and your team have been working on was very successful and your boss was pleased. Friday after work, you and your co-workers go out for a few drinks and pleasant conversation. At Saturday's hockey game, your kid scores the winning goal, and you just happen to capture a video on your iPhone to show all your buddies. As the weekend rolls on, you find yourself accomplishing household tasks with energy. Come Sunday, you're excited to get the kids off to another week of school and get to work on the next project your employer asked your help with.

Monday morning, you arrive at work early. As you enter your office building, you see a piece of trash on the sidewalk, pick it up, and place it in the nearby trash can, never missing a stride as you enter the building.

As you arrive at work desk, you see that a co-workers on whom you rely heavily throughout the day has a very long face. Being concerned, you ask gently, trying not to pry, to see what is bothering them. You now hear about the family blowup that took place with the in-laws, the rotten time this person had all weekend doing chores because the spouse was out on a trip with friends, the kids are not doing well in school, and on and on.

Attitude Is Highly Contagious

Your first thought after hearing all this is, "What the heck did I get myself into, asking them what's going on?!" Then you try to find a way to change the subject. Next, you probably try to look at your phone to see if you can say there is an important call that you have to take, while thinking, "Oh boy, glad I am not that person!"

So why does this happen? It's because you don't want anyone to rain on your happy parade. It's because most people try to avoid negativity, especially when they are not in a bad mood.

You extract yourself from the conversation, shake your head, and find yourself a little less energetic. "I have to work with this person all week!" you think to yourself. Then you catch yourself with a sigh, and your shoulders sag a bit.

Subconsciously, you let your co-worker's attitude affect yours. This happens all the time, probably more than you think. Even the most powerful positive thinkers are affected by attitude because it's so darn contagious, like an infectious disease. Your attitude, whether positive or negative, affects everyone you interact with, all day long.

> Your attitude, whether positive or negative, affects everyone you interact with.

Sharing Attitude by Means of a Handshake

Over time, I've witnessed some interesting scenarios. First, some people try to copy others who have a great attitude. It's the "I want what they're drinking" theory, mimicking others they are envious of. When you see someone with lots of energy, that bounce in their step, that look in their eye, your first thought is to hang with that person and maybe it will rub off. Maybe I can be like them if I study what they are doing.

Well, you're right! You can self-teach, or mimic, a positive attitude.

To demonstrate just how contagious attitude can be, I use this experiment almost every day. I find it interesting to watch how people shake hands when greeting each other. The attitude each person demonstrates in this gesture is completely contagious. So not only do I shake hands as a form of saying hello, but I watch how people greet one another.

When I recruit and coach student athletes for our baseball team, I'm basically dealing with 18- to 22-year-old males. They're great athletes, and they usually have a good-size ego. I try to interact and converse with them not like I am their parent, but as their coach and mentor.

It is important to see what type of personality they have, which usually is evident in the first 30 seconds of an interaction. I can't tell you how many times I have met a player who does the "three shake, knuckle bump, hug" greeting. Admittedly, I usually have no idea what I'm doing, and usually just follow along, trying to copy what the 20-year-old shows me. It's a handshake he and his peers probably do 50 times a day.

The player will say, "Coach! Gimme some skin!" and continue to shake hands with me three or four different ways, then knuckle bump my fist, and finish with a hug.

> People mimic other's movements and attitudes.

Like clockwork, I copy and follow right along.

There's also something I love to do when greeting someone for the first time. In our society, we typically extend our hand and engage in a three-second shake. But what happens when you use those seconds to also slightly pull your counterpart toward you and tap them on the shoulder? Well, they tap you back. Every time. They copy you. They might feel a bit uncomfortable, but they do it anyway.

How about that potentially awkward moment in the greeting process when the person goes in for the hug? You copy them and the attitude they bring and you hug right back. Ever been in that "hug" situation where both parties are hesitant? You both go for the shake, then one half-heartily starts the hug, so now you switch gears to hug mode, only to have the person fake you out and go back to the shake. It can be quite amusing as you copy every move they make.

These things happen because people tend to mimic the movements and the attitudes of others. Someone who shakes your hand with the knuckle bump or the shoulder tap is demonstrating some energy, with a bit of an aggressive attitude, and that person will dominate the greeting. And you don't want to be the negative Nellie, so you copy them, even if you don't quite feel the same way.

Change Your Thought Process to One of Positivity

Just as you can catch other people's attitudes, other people can catch yours. When you show up to work with the Monday morning blues, you affect everyone.

> A big part of being a leader is how you present yourself.

A depressed look on your face, a slow shuffle in your walk—these telegraph to the entire office that you really don't want any part of being there. Others can feel your energy, your vibe, and your attitude, which can infect everyone negatively.

A big part of being a leader is how you present yourself. The people around you will follow your lead, whether positive or negative. In fact, if you've built the trust and loyalty needed to be a successful leader, your employees will follow you more than you think. They often assume that since you're in charge, there is a bit of pressure to follow you. If you're upset, they become upset. If you're happy, then they too will be happy.

You *Choose* Your Attitude

You can only fool the people you surround yourself with for so long. You may have heard the term "Fake it till you make it." Although there may be times when you have to pretend to be positive when you really don't feel like it, it's not possible to trick your employees over longer periods of time. Remember, most of your team probably knows what makes you tick, especially if you worked hard to build relationships with them. If you're not genuine with your attitude and don't believe in what you're preaching, people will eventually recognize this. You can only fake it for so long. A false sense of enthusiasm will soon be exposed and can lead to you losing creditability as a leader.

Let me paint a picture of something that happens quite frequently in my role as a college baseball coach. The student athletes who play a Division I sport tend to have busy schedules: a morning strength workout prior to classes, then three or four classes, study hall time, and meetings with professors. Usually, once afternoon hits, they gravitate to their respective practice facilities and engage in a three-hour practice.

Those in the workforce experience similarly busy schedules. We get the kids off to school, get ready for work, check the calendar for meetings, work on the big project due at the end of the week, take conference calls, only to realize it's 4 p.m., and the kids need to be picked up.

And it usually doesn't end there—afterschool practice sessions, dinner preparation, getting kids to bed, then, if you're lucky, time to rest your mind.

Young adults in college may not entirely understand the significance of these responsibilities, but the intense schedules of student athletes can be a building block for their future.

So it's extremely important for me, as their coach, to help them understand the value of focusing on the task at hand. Any wasted time can deter the team from improving, learning a new play, or simply working better together.

As head coach, my role is not only to teach, but to mentor and lead as well. Most days I too have a busy schedule. Long meetings, workshops, NCAA rules education, and more can all happen prior to gathering my group for a three-hour practice.

On any given day, prior to practice, my athletic director might chew me out because the program is way over budget and I have to find a way to raise that quickly. Then a recruit I've spent time pursuing for months might call to break the news that he has decided to attend a rival university. Next, I find out from a professor that one of our student athletes has been goofing off in class, and that professor is quite upset with him. Damn, there goes our team image, I think. While walking across campus, in comes a call to my cell phone from a resident director that another young adult has been disruptive after quiet hours in the dorms.

You get my drift: many distractions occur day in and day out. If I choose to show up to practice with a negative attitude influenced by all the day's events, it will affect the players around me. Because daily issues can take a toll, I learned how to turn my mood into a positive one quickly, so when I head into that office meeting or field practice, I refocus one hundred percent of my energy on my players and team. If not, the group will see and feel my bad attitude. If I spend that three-hour practice window yelling commands and pointing out all the failures, I will lose the group that day. Their focus will not be on the skills needed to improve during practice but on the process of "surviving" the day. No one wants to be around me when I'm full of negativity, which will ultimately keep the players from being in the right frame of mind to focus on trying to improve their skills.

> There is a big difference between "faking"
> your attitude and learning how to refo-
> cus your attitude.

Don't get me wrong—there's always room for correction and discussions when working together as a group. Yet the outcome has to be one of positivity. The valuable time we have together can be adversely affected, leading us to fail to accomplish what we set out to do. There is a big difference between "faking" your attitude and learning how to refocus your attitude.

If you choose to allow the daily grind to affect your attitude in a negative way, it will certainly result in poor outcomes within your organization. Do your best to master the technique of willing yourself to have a positive attitude. This is not always easy, but there are many ways to learn to use breathing, mindfulness, and other techniques to accomplish this.

> Do your best to master the technique
> of willing yourself to have a positive
> attitude.

Do *you* want to be around you when dealing with negative situations? Take a moment to observe yourself in these tough moments. How would you like to see yourself in times of crisis management, when things are not going so well? Can you envision watching a movie, with you as the lead character, and observe your attitude and behavior?

And as difficult as it can be some days, having the ability to find one simple, small thing to be positive about can go a long way. Remember, your attitude is highly contagious!

Be a Grinder, and Deal with Setbacks

Leaders often find it difficult to remain constantly positive. In fact, it isn't possible to be on the positive train all day, every day. There are always going to be setbacks, failures, lost accounts, and problems that pile up that can lead your attitude into a negative place. You are human, and that means you'll experience the many emotions that arise from both success and failure. It's okay to have a moment when you might let some negative emotions creep in due to a failure.

However, when you expect these challenges to happen and refuse to back down or give up, you'll find ways to change your attitude to a more positive one. We've all heard the glass-half-empty or half-full theory: the optimist will always look for the positive, not the negative, in a given situation. You need to develop the skill to look deep enough when posed with an issue, to channel your thoughts and energy into an optimistic approach. When you master this, you will certainly become a better leader. You will be more pleasant to be around, and your employees and teammates will gravitate toward you. When this magnetic effect happens, people are more willing to trust and listen to your ideas, and will ultimately follow your lead.

Fight through the "Muck"

Realize that there will be bad days, with failures, missed sales, and team losses. You have to address these issues, but if you can acquire the skill to derive a positive from a negative situation, others will follow. You *chose* to be the leader, the CEO, the head coach, the boss. That entails the responsibility of leading your group. Your leadership can only be long term if you show up on a consistent basis with an attitude that is infectious in a good way.

In the workplace, this can have a huge impact on success or failure. Take a moment to envision the banking world for an example. Imagine you drive up to the window at your bank to make a deposit, and the teller greets you with an enthusiastic smile and a hello. As she completes the transaction, she not only says thank you, but notices from your account information that your birthday is a week away, so she wishes you an early happy birthday. When you pull away, you feel better; the teller's nice personality warmed you. You are satisfied that you conduct business with this bank and appreciate the experience you had.

> Teach your people to communicate with
> positive energy and attitude.

Fast-forward a few months. Now you're in the market to refinance your house and are looking for a mortgage. Your first stop will undoubtably be the same bank because you feel good about the place. You might even decide to pay a slightly higher interest rate because you gravitate toward the great customer service from this financial institution. All because a teller took the time to have a great attitude.

Of course, this can go both ways. That same scenario would be quite different if the teller was having a bad day, and her attitude reflected that when you stopped by that day.

Find a moment to communicate in a positive way. Teach your people to communicate with positive energy and attitude. It might be at your darkest hour or during crisis management, but that is when employees look to the top. They want someone to follow during tough times. My former college coach taught me a saying: "Tough times don't last, but tough people do."

We frequently speak in the sports world of "tough people." True toughness isn't about how loud you are or how much you pump your chest and posture at the opposing team. The toughest ones have focus, lock in to the task at hand, and above all have an attitude that is not only positive, but contagious. They understand the importance of following a set of standards and values that an organization has established to lead to a strong culture.

Remember, a handshake is all it takes to have someone begin to follow your lead.

Coach's Challenge

1. What person in your life do you try to be like because of their infectious attitude?

2. How can you establish a routine to get rid of the Monday morning blues?

3. When has your attitude affected your image in a positive or negative way?

4. Who around you is really a "tough" person?

5. How can you find a way to rub off positively on the people on your team?

4

The Communicator Wins

Communication is one of the most important leadership traits for bringing people together within an organization. Most people want a direct path to follow, with guidance along the way, in order to feel they've accomplished a task or an organizational goal. The ability to communicate is essential if you want to lead. A leader must find ways to energize, motivate, and sometimes deliver unwanted news though various means of communication.

The First and Best Form of Communication

In today's world, there are many forms of communications at our disposal. Of course, we can still have a good old face-to-face conversation with an individual or a group of people. However, as times have changed and technology has grown, so have the ways we communicate. Nowadays, we can write, email, text, and even post information on social media to get a message to someone.

Of all the ways to communicate, there really is no substitute for in-person verbal communication. Not everyone feels comfortable with this, but if you want to be a good leader, you must hone this skill.

Think back to your school days of being forced to do oral presentations in front of the entire class. Teachers have always recognized the value of public speaking and how it can be an effective tool as we grow and mature.

> There really is no substitute for in-person
> verbal communication.

Oral communication provides a lot more feedback about how our interaction is going than do other communication avenues. Facial expressions, emotion, body language, and eye contact are hard to replicate when sending a text or an email. In an attempt to mimic this, people add well-known symbols to their written communications to represent emotions, hence the term "emojis" that is now common in our everyday vocabulary.

Surely many of us have received an email that takes valuable time to decipher the intended tone and context:

"What did she mean by that word?"

"Is he mad at me?'

"Do they want me to do this right now?"

It can be quite difficult to deliver a message when you remove the ability to show emotion while conversing. Many wires can become crossed, leading to miscommunication.

One of my pet peeves is this exact scenario. When there is a question that needs to be addressed, I force myself to place and return phone calls. Time and time again, I leave a voice mail when there is no answer, only to receive a text message in return, and then the conversation continues via texting. I fail to gain valuable information to assess the topic, such as their emotion and reaction to my thoughts and rebuttals. If I am able to read emotions in a face-to-face communication, I can rethink my ideas based on input and dialogue. Conversely, without that I lose the ability to pivot my thoughts in order to become better prepared.

"Hey, Dave. Let me bounce an idea off you." If Dave writes back his thoughts, I can certainly gain his perspective. But if he winces or rolls his eyes or shows positive body language, I gain so much more insight into his true thoughts, which helps me to decipher how to proceed with my idea.

One of my greatest fears in tackling this book is that of communication. Get me up in front of a group to discuss leadership and my energy and enthusiasm are on full display, and I can really get my point across. But even when my brain knows what I want to say, getting these thoughts down on paper with emotion proves to be a challenge. How can I grab my audience without being able to do what I am most comfortable with: talking? Writing may not be my greatest strength, but talking through a conversation is. To that point, I hope the written copy of this book isn't dwarfed by the success the audio copy will have!

Become Comfortable Communicating in Person

Good leaders strive to be fair and truthful. However, poor leaders often lack the ability to communicate well in person and don't like being in uncomfortable situations. Thus they often choose certain forms of communication specifically to avoid direct contact when delivering tough news. They may like one-on-one meetings when sharing the good news about a raise or promotion, but they send an email when letting someone go. This makes it difficult for them to earn the respect of the team and can make it difficult to gain the trust and loyalty a leader needs from the entire organization.

Think of how we learn in school and our ability to communicate with teachers and professors. Good teachers recognize when the class is drifting out of focus and employ tactics to reengage pupils. They have the ability to hold attention through communication. Even when the topic might seem mundane, a good communicator continues to hold the interest of the group. In a class or a work meeting lasting an hour, most attendees will only be locked in probably 20% of that time.

Quality educators and experienced leaders in the office develop the necessary means to increase attention and hold focus for extended periods of time. Modulating your voice or adjusting your volume can bring your audience back into focus on the topic being discussed. Keeping everyone engaged and focused can lead to a productive learning environment.

We All Love a Good Storyteller

Have you ever met someone with the ability to tell a really good story? Someone who you really lock into when they speak? Great communicators are great storytellers as well.

> Great communicators are great storytellers as well.

I have a great friend named Dan Olson whom I consider to be a terrific storyteller. I met Dan years ago, when I was running baseball camps while coaching at Manhattan College in New York. His son, Jackson, attended my camp. Dan talked to me about his job as a sales representative for Rawlings Sporting Goods Company, one of the leading companies in baseball products.

Dan wasn't pushing to get my business; rather he offered his help if I ever wanted to look into using his company for our baseball needs. Over time, I got to know Dan well, and eventually I signed a contract with him and Rawlings. There are other companies out there whose products are just as good, but I found Dan's personality and charisma refreshing and I wanted to be associated with him.

In fact, this is a phenomenon that happens quite frequently in the world of business. People don't just buy the product; they tend to buy the person selling the product, so a confident sales representative with a quality personality has a distinct advantage. At most levels of competition, there is little difference in product performance. However, when choosing between Land's End or Eddie Bauer, Chevy or Ford, UPS or FedEx, most of us eventually make a decision based on the connection we make with the salesperson.

> People don't buy the product; they tend
> to buy the person selling that product.

Dan's storytelling is legendary. He has the ability to share a message, either fictional or factual, that captures your attention. He doesn't speak too long or forget a key detail that leaves a gap in the story. He uses his emotions, laughter, enthusiasm, even anger in his body language and facial expressions. This keeps his audience captivated and hanging on every word.

Dan is fun to be around and willing to communicate to build trust and loyalty with others. In turn, I trust in what he does for work and who he works for. I have been a loyal Rawlings customer for over 20 years. His storytelling and his personality fostered my longstanding relationship with the business he worked for.

Over the course of our working relationship, I was approached multiple times by competitors to switch my business.

I would hear how their bats, baseballs, gloves, or uniforms are much better and told I should be using their products. Dan has since retired from Rawlings, yet I signed another multi-year agreement with the company because he set the groundwork, through his personality, for me to be a lifelong loyal Rawlings customer. Even though it's been a long time since Dan was my sales rep, my bond with him is still strong.

Communication Pays Off

During a recent business trip, I had a bit of time to kill at the Atlanta International Airport. Usually I pull into the rental facility like a NASCAR driver and then run through terminals desperately looking for the right gate, hoping to make it on time.

But this time my meetings had ended early, which meant I didn't have to rush, and in fact I had four hours to burn. What a great opportunity to catch up on some work! Part of this week-long business trip had taken me to New Jersey, where I spend an afternoon with my publisher, John Wiley & Sons, to discuss this very book! We laid out a plan for me to finish writing, along with the process of marketing and editing the work to get it ready for release.

I left New Jersey and headed to Atlanta for several days of meetings and recruiting future student-athletes before preparing to return home to Florida. I felt energized, ready to dive into the tasks the publishers assigned to me.

My four-hour layover at the airport promised to be valuable time to knock out some writing. I sought a quiet spot to grab a bite to eat and sit with my laptop. I noticed a cool-looking wine bar with what seemed to be a decent menu. I noticed a few open tables that looked like a good place to plop down and dive into my writing assignment.

As I entered the restaurant, I noticed a display showcasing specialty wines and a sign that read, "Quality wines to sample."

Since I had just spent seven long days in publishing meetings, coupled with recruiting baseball players in the hot Atlanta sun, this caught my attention.

I also noticed a waitress at the front of the restaurant whose body language and facial expression seemed to be broadcasting, "I really don't want to working here tonight." But I proceeded anyway and kindly asked her about trying a good red wine.

"Hey there, I like the idea of sampling, so how does this work?" I said.

"Sorry, no samples. Do you want to order?" she replied.

As I scratched my head in confusion and turned to read the sign again, I decided, in light of my good mood, simply to shrug it off.

"Sure, how about you pick me a winner from the choices you have." I said with a bit of energy.

"ID?" she grumbled.

"Oh, you think I look too young! Well, thank you for that!"

"No, that's not it. I have to ID everyone, or I lose my job." Not the response I was hoping for.

She then picked up the bottle closest to her and poured me a glass of pinot noir. As she removed the cork with her fingers, I noticed there was probably not enough left for a full glass, so I figured she would open a fresh one. Not only did she give me a glass only three-quarters full, but I could see sediment floating in the glass. Surely she would dump this, or even attempt to top it off from a new bottle.

"$14.00." She held her hand out.

I had planned on also ordering a sandwich, but I thought maybe I should hold off, drink my wine with floaties in it, and try to find another restaurant.

When she handed me the credit card slip to sign, I added a modest $1 tip. I hate not to tip because I understand servers rely on tips for a good portion of their salary, but her attitude didn't seem to merit more.

I moved to an open table and got on my laptop to write, but I couldn't focus because I still was thinking about how that person could easily have been friendlier. Still, I didn't want that to change my mood; I was excited to dive into my computer and to be heading home. So, I took a sip of my wine, decided the bitterness of the stale bottle was not pleasing, and quickly scanned the area for another place to kill off some time.

As I walked by a garbage can, I disposed of the plastic cup and remaining wine. I spotted a Seafood restaurant in the distance. Figuring this wasn't the best location to get a great piece of fish, my first thought was to take a pass. As I strolled closer, a waitress saw me glancing at the menu and called out cheerfully, "Hey there, sweetheart! How about you take a load off your feet and join us. We have the best food in Atlanta!"

Pretty big boast, but she seemed like a fun person. So I decided to give it a try and find a quiet place to sit down.

"My name is Shonda, and I will be personally taking care of you. You look like you have some work to do before your flight, so how about I find a good spot, next to an outlet, to charge that laptop in your hand."

I sat down and fired up my computer.

Shonda quickly returned. "What can I get you to drink?"

As I scanned the wine list I began to say, "Well, I was kinda in the mood for another glass of wine. How about the . . ."

Shonda interjected, "Sweetheart, you want the merlot. It's my most popular and I will personally take it off your bill if you don't like it."

"But before I grab that glass, can I see your ID please? You look way too young to be drinking and I just want to make sure so I don't get in trouble," she said with a wink. Given my recent negative experience with the previous restaurant, I couldn't help but chuckle.

I now had about three hours before boarding my plane and decided to try to get some writing done on my book.

Shonda brought my wine and asked if I wanted to order some food. I asked if she had any food recommendations since she had been so helpful with the wine.

"Baby, you definitely want the blackened salmon. It's my personal favorite!"

"Sounds like a winner, Shonda. Also, I have a few hours, so don't feel like you have to rush it.

"You got it, Steve. Take as long as you like. Give me a wave of your hand if you need anything at all."

How did she know my name? Ah yes, she memorized it when she saw my ID. Now that's a pretty good trick.

As she walked away with my order, I really felt energized to write. Shonda's great energy made me feel good and loosened me up a bit after a long week.

After a few minutes, Shonda checked in with an update on when my fish would arrive. "Wow, Steve, you look deep in thought, buried behind that computer. Must be an important presentation."

"Well actually, I'm attempting to write a book and have a deadline to finish up a few chapters."

"A book? How cool!" Her voice surged with energy. "I've been working as a waitress for 29 years and boy could I write a book about what I've seen!"

She looked so young that the 29 years comment surprised me. I couldn't help but think she must be pretty good at her job to have been at it so long.

"How about another glass of my famous wine, Mr. Steve?"

"Shonda, if I have another, my readers might think I'm nuts, so I better stop at one," I joked.

I went back to writing on my laptop. I stared at the screen, wondering which topic to tackle next. I looked my notes on which chapters remained to be completed. Then, it hit me. "Communicate" seemed to jump off the page. Shonda had given me one of those "light bulb" moments. She was a great communicator, with charisma and an infectious personality that made me feel welcomed and comfortable.

As she arrived with my food, she said, "Hope you enjoy! It's my favorite."

I glanced down at a small piece of salmon a side of broccoli. Unfortunately the fish was overdone and dry and the broccoli was soggy and mushy.

Shonda came by to ask how the meal was.

"Great, Shonda. Awesome recommendation!" I told her. I didn't have the heart to mention the state of what appeared to be a microwaved meal. I hadn't had any expectations walking in, so it really didn't bother me. I knew it was worth it to meet Shonda.

I reflected how important it is to be the ultimate communicator when serving food. Shonda's attitude, communication skills, and personality all led to me feeling excited, happy, energized, and motivated, despite the unpleasant meal. Great leaders understand the importance of communication, and Shonda had just given me a great example of how powerful this trait can be.

Time flew by as I continued to write, and it was time to get going to make my flight home. Being a pro at her job, Shonda recognized this and quickly brought the bill.

"Thanks, Steve. I hope you have great success with your book."

"Shonda, you have no idea how you've helped me. For that, I thank you!" "I'm going to write my email address on the bill, so if this book ever gets off the ground, I want to send you a copy. Your personality had a great influence on my day, and helped give me an idea for my book."

She blushed. "Well, thank you, Steve. I just love my job and getting the chance to meet people."

She left the bill and we said our final goodbyes. I finished filling out my credit card slip and came to the tip line. Since I was using the company card on school business, I had limits on the amount I could tip. After I gave the maximum allowed, I slipped a $20 bill into the black receipt holder, and wrote my address on the slip as promised. She had certainly earned that tip!

The Power of a Personality

Shonda further proved to me what I already believed in: there are a few skills necessary to be a great communicator.

First, you need to have a positive personality that people will gravitate toward. As discussed earlier, the attitude you bring to your day is highly contagious and others will definitely notice. Even when someone is not in the best of moods, they will seek out someone who has a positive vibe about them. This goes hand and hand with someone who also possesses a positive personality.

Personality is a combination of a person's physical, mental, social, and emotional characteristics. It can manifest in how you act, verbalize, use expressions, and even how you dress. With a great personality, you have the ability to take a vital step in leading a group or team by connecting with others. When people in a group feel "connected" to the leader, they tend to develop a sense of trust and respect. This, in turn, will aid in the groups' ability to sustain long-term success and demonstrates just how powerful a positive personality can be.

Shonda's infectious personality was such a strong influence that she lured me into an average restaurant with mediocre food and I still had a great experience. Her personality led to a reward—it motivated me to leave her a good tip.

Charisma

Another skill a great communicator holds is having charisma, attracting people to their ideas, issues, or conversations. Others become curious and want to study and even mimic their moves. Their magic touch of leadership inspires those around them and can build enthusiasm within an organization. Charisma aids in the ability to communicate, which leads to building trust and loyalty with the people they engage with. Remember my buddy Dan? His skill as a communicator and storyteller, combined with captivating charisma, led to my loyalty and investment in what he was selling.

> Good communicators demonstrate the
> ability to have others believe in them.

A leader has to bring a positive, infectious charismatic attitude each and every day. Good communicators demonstrate the ability to have others believe in them. The quality is genuine, with no hidden fake ideas. A good leader will also understand when they are talking too much, stumbling through a lesson or meeting. This will lose the audience, and can lead to people in the group losing their focus.

A great example of this is when you coach your own kids. How many parents out there have said the same things over and over again to their kids, only to get little to no response. Yet, bring in another voice saying the exact same thing, and the response is immediate. So many times a parent has asked me to do a baseball lesson with a young player, and then dad or mom exclaims, "Well, I said the same thing, but they won't listen to me!" I guess this is why it can be difficult to coach your own kids. It's a good thing I didn't attempt to coach my daughters in ice hockey, but my excuse was that I'm a baseball coach and don't know how to skate!

Charisma is a helpful tool to become a better communicator, but remember to be genuine and recognize when to back down in a conversation.

Don't Dominate the Conversation

The last skill I want to address here is the ability to listen. Good communicators listen to others, especially when they're talking about themselves. This proves to be difficult at times, because most people feel they need to add to a conversation in order to be a part of it. You must develop the ability to refrain from jumping into someone's conversation, especially when the person you are engaged with is speaking about themselves.

Most people want to talk about themselves. They like to share how well their kids or spouses are performing in school, sports, or work. This isn't a bad thing; it's human nature to brag about things going well in your life. We can all think of examples of conversations with someone who's talking about just how well little Jimmy is doing in school, while we're searching for the quickest exit strategy.

> Be a good listener, even when you have to fake it.

When you first meet someone, or even when you're around familiar faces of friends, colleagues, or clients, you need to ask them about themselves. Everyone glows when you ask about their kids or other family members. This gives the person a sense of calm, as you show that you genuinely want to hear how things are going for them: "Hey Jen, how're those great ball players of yours doing?"

Also, when someone asks about something in my world, I try to pivot the conversation quickly back to them: "Enough about me, Jen, I want to hear about your kids."

When you acquire this skill, people tend to be more comfortable with you in conversation when you're cultivating a relationship. Be a good listener, even when you have to fake it. This tactic, combined with charisma, is vital to long-term success in communication, allowing you to connect with an individual. Possessing the ability to put yourself second in a conversation, not dominating it with self-promotion, leads you to converse in a genuine way. In turn, you get to close the deal, the sale, the account, the recruit, and the gap in the relationship.

On that day in Atlanta, Shonda connected with me and we had an engaging conversation. After the time we spent in that seafood restaurant, she closed out my bill and collected her reward. This is reminiscent of our earlier discussion about the more you give, the more you get in return. Shonda gave me a lot that day, in the way of a natural life lesson. She reminded me of the importance of human connection and effective communication.

I can't wait to run into her again so I can give her a better tip.

Coach's Challenge

1. What form of communication do you feel most comfortable with?
2. Practice engaging in a conversation with someone where you ask three questions and you listen to the answers, without responding about yourself.
3. What is a personality trait you feel comfortable with?
4. What personality trait do you want to improve on?

5

I Always Got Hits Because My Shoelaces Were Tucked In

Luck: we're all guilty of relying on it. We use luck in a multitude of ways to give reasons why or why not something works out for us.

Luck:
1. The things that happen to a person because of chance: the accidental way things happen without being planned
2. Success or failure apparently brought by chance rather than through one's own actions (Source: dictionary.com)

Sorry to break it to you, but there is no such thing as luck defining the outcome of something we hope will happen. Yet we fall for this mentality time and time again because blaming luck for a positive or negative outcome is a much easier path. It provides built-in excuses, allowing us to shirk responsibility or to deny credit to someone to whom we might not want to give credit: an employee sealed the big account or a player got the big hit in the game because of some cosmic force that visited from the heavens. But the truth is that belief in luck does not dictate the outcome. Rather, when you have a concise plan and stick to a routine that has proven to work, you increase the odds to be successful more times than not.

Follow Planned Routines

When it comes to preparation, having a positive and strict routine can be a vital link to a successful outcome. This is why we practice, both on the playing field and in the office. You wouldn't go into a huge sales meeting with a potential client, where a Power-Point presentation is needed to describe how your company will be the right choice to land the account, without studying for the presentation. We have been taught to prepare as much as we can for situations in case things don't quite go our way. That's when we go into crisis management mode, forcing us to pivot from our set plan of action to try to fix the situation. We practice this in order to get the meeting, game, or conversation back on track.

So, we are taught to come up with a solid, prepared routine when we set out to accomplish a task. The groundwork we lay prior to a particular meeting, presentation, or game will lead to better outcomes over a sustained period of time. Think of the Boy Scout motto: "Be prepared."

Wasting Time on What You Can't Influence

When I played baseball in college, I was convinced that if I followed a certain routine, it would lead to me being a better player. This approach can be highly successful; routines in sports and the workplace can have a multitude of positive outcomes. It can build confidence when completing a task. It can make a person comfortable in certain situations.

The problem was that I tried to create routines around desired outcomes over which I had no control, as opposed to outcomes that I could influence. Focusing on things I couldn't control led me either to blame these ridiculous routines for my failures, or praise them when I had success. Many people make the same mistake.

My routine had to do with my shoelaces.

Yes, shoelaces. How silly does that sound now? I believed if I followed a certain routine where I laced my shoes a certain way, the baseball gods would allow me to be successful.

One day prior to a game as I laced up my spikes, I saw that my laces had larger than normal loops hanging out. It must have been the way I tied them that day. My initial thought was if those loops ever hooked on my other foot's spike, I would go for a tumble, therefore not getting a jump on a fly ball or being able to steal the base. So I tucked the loops inside my shoes. There, solved that problem, I thought.

Well, that day I had one of my best games. If you've ever played a sport, you will understand that some days you feel you can do no wrong. This was one of those days. Ball players know it can go south in a real hurry, where the baseball can look like an aspirin coming at you when it is pitched for you to hit.

Not this day, though. Every pitch thrown to me looked like a beach ball. I went 4 for 5 with 2 doubles! And I had 2 great defensive catches in center field. I couldn't wait to get back to the ball park the next day to keep the hot streak going.

So as the next game rolled around, I made darn sure that I laced up my spikes the same way. It seemed imperative that I tuck in those laces again. But not because it would help prevent me from tripping. Clearly it was going to lead to my playing better and getting hits!

On this day, however, I was not able to repeat a 4–5 day at the plate, yet I still collected a few hits. I became convinced my routine of tucking in those laces led to my success at the plate as a hitter. So, as the season went on, day in and day out I continued to tuck in those laces to follow my routine.

However, my hot streak quickly ended; 0–4 with 3 strike-outs soon followed. Then another poor game, followed by another. Soon my coach sat my butt on the bench and started the other outfielder.

What was going on? I was still tucking in the laces, so why no hits?

Looking back, I see what a complete waste of time this was. I convinced myself this silly routine led to my success. Yet I had no control over this "lucky" thing.

Control the Controllables

My success was not due to unbelievably good fortune or because of a lucky shoelace superstition but because I was focused, comfortable, and confident with my approach when batting. I just happened to be well prepared during this time frame. My hot streak quickly came to an end, like most good streaks do. Routines are a vital component to sustain success, but my routine of tucking in the laces was not responsible for my success or failure as a hitter. A lack of confidence and proper preparation also added to my failure. Doubting one's routine can certainly lead to doubting one's ability, but routines have to contain specific habits and customs that directly relate to a successful outcome. We all experience ups and downs at the workplace and on the playing field. It should be expected.

But what if I focused on preparing for the game better instead of worrying about my shoelaces and the superstition of luck?

What if I took a few more batting practice swings, or studied the opposing pitcher more? My wasted valuable time clearly led to my failure to properly prepare. I spent precious moments relying on something I can't control, when I could have focused on controllable moments.

So, again, I hate to be the bearer of bad news, but there is no such thing as luck, other than what we create for ourselves. Sometimes things don't go our way due to numerous possible reasons, but not because of luck.

It's Fun to Be a "Little Stitious"

One of my favorite television series is *The Office*, with Steve Carell as Michael Scott. If you love good comedy and have not watched the series, I highly recommend it. In one of Michael's classic talks with Dwight Schrute, the office salesperson and part-time beet farmer, along with another one of the hilarious characters, they discuss how the paper company they work for was having bad luck in solidifying sales. Michael describes his lack of belief in luck:

"I'm not superstitious, but I'm a little stitious."

I have this quote framed and hanging in my office and use the line quite often to remind my players or work groups that, when seeking success, they should laugh a little about the notion of relying on supernatural ideas over which we have no control.

> Build off your wins, and find ways to con-
> stantly improve from your failures.

Another way to look at it is that you create your own luck. Positive outcomes happen when we focus on the things over which we have control—the routines that have substance and allow us to be better prepared for success. All too often, people will credit or blame things totally out of their control: an employee landed a huge account because of a lucky tie, or an athlete scored a touchdown because of the wristband he chose to wear.

> You create your own luck.

When things don't go in your favor, you start to look for excuses, instead of focusing on how to best improve on your failures. Things won't go your way all the time, but not because you left your lucky charm at home that day. Maybe we lost an account to a competitor because the sales pitch was not a solid one, not because we drank the wrong brand of coffee that morning.

This reminds us of the valuable lesson to focus on what you can control, not what you can't. Believe me, as a college baseball coach I have attempted to control things like umpires, opposing coaches, and even the weather. It doesn't work! Do not look for excuses about why things didn't go your way. Look for why something didn't work, then find a path to better navigate it the next time. Use your setbacks as a motivator and a teacher. Build off your wins, and look for ways to constantly improve from your failures. Evaluate how you work outside your comfort zone, try something different, and recognize the positive changes that come from your pivots.

> Focus on what you can control, not what
> you can't.

So, don't waste time blaming luck for outcomes. It's a long-standing human tradition, but luck has nothing to do with our successes and failures.

However, throwing a penny on the ground and hoping it lands heads up can be a fun little diversion! Remember, you can be a "little stitious."

Coach's Challenge

1. What routine can you draw up that can lead to a positive outcome?

2. Can you name a recent moment where you and your team blamed luck for the negative outcome of a situation?

3. When was your team able to "pivot" from something that was not going your way, allowing everyone to get back on track?

4. List three things your group has control over each day.

6

Leaders Lead the Way

We have discussed how a leader's attitude and positive outlook can be such a fuel to the organization he or she is part of. Those traits and values can dictate what type of leadership style you might have. Many people engage in studying leadership and its various styles numerous times. I really believe there are three basic leadership styles and you can choose one of them or a combination: dictator, servant, and empowerment leadership.

Let me share a fictitious story with you to demonstrate the dangerous type of dictator leadership.

John and His New Boss

John is excited because today his new boss, David, will be introduced to the entire company. After weeks of rumors and chatter, the new sheriff is in town! As John gets ready that morning, his wife is doing her best to get two half-awake kids downstairs to the breakfast table and off to school for the day.

"Hey, honey, need any help?" John says halfheartedly.

She gives her shifty smile as to send a message: " Yeah, right, big help you are."

But, being the keen leader of the family, she recognizes that John's mind is in another place. They talked the previous night about the introduction of David, the new CEO, coming on board.

John works at a company of roughly 90 employees, all hardworking blue-collar types. Although they're worn down from long hours and are hoping someday they might be awarded raises for their efforts, everyone tends to get along. Despite the usual office cliques, there was nothing that would fracture the organization.

In his upper-management role, John is in charge of the sales and marketing team, responsible, first and foremost, for bringing in the accounts. He and his team are very proud of their accomplishments and work well together to lure, cultivate, and close accounts. They have a core group of loyal clients they built over time. John also has responsibilities to market the company and build community relations. He wears many different hats throughout the course of the day, and really loves the responsibility he has earned over the years of employment.

John kissed his wife, hugged his twin daughters, and left the house 10 minutes earlier than usual, excited to start his day. His mind began to anticipate the initial meeting with the new boss. What type of person is David, he wondered. Can he really fulfill those promises of salary increases and a good work environment? Would he and his wife want to get to know all of the employees outside the office? Should John and his wife invite them for dinner?

John sat front row in the companywide 9 a.m. meeting, where David was about to address the crowd. Coffee and donuts were on hand, which was something new. John took two. Power breakfast, he thought.

David came from a rival company and held a similar management role there. What struck John and a few others who had chatted with him the previous week via a phone conversation was David's willingness to move from company to company so often. It was known David had recently been at two companies prior to arriving at theirs.

As David began his introductory talk, John's initial enthusiasm began to wane. The tone was not like the time they had met a few weeks earlier, when David addressed upper management during his in-person interview. That day, David was filled with energy and spoke swiftly, addressing the people and explaining the things he had done well, along with challenges to be faced together. That day, the management team had left David's interview with optimism for the future of their company if he were to be chosen as their next leader.

Today was different, right from his opening remarks. John saw a man standing at the podium with a different message. David's speech revolved around his first 90 days. In that window, David made it clear he was going to observe, with little to no interaction, then make decisions and changes as he saw fit. Of course, he wasn't going to be entirely alone. He had formed a senior leadership team of two individuals who would advise him during this 90-day evaluation. As John sat and listened, he had an uneasy sensation, as did the other 88 or so employees, who felt the same pressure as John.

David announced that his two team members were Susan and Nathan, the same two upper-management people that were on the search committee for his hiring.

"Wait," John thought. "Did this just happen? Did the two individuals who had a hand in hiring David receive a promotion?"

As the meeting concluded, he noticed the entire room looking confused and feeling puzzled. No one knew if they should huddle and discuss, leave quickly, or hang around to introduce themselves to David.

John watched as Bob, one of his co-workers and more outgoing sales managers, made his way through the room to offer a hand and introduction to David. John tried not to stare, but he wanted to see if he noticed anything about David's body language. As Bob came close to David, saying hello and extending a polite handshake, John watched as David greeted him with a quick nod and continued to fold his notes and pack up his laptop. No return handshake. Poor Bob, John thought. There he was, probably the most outgoing person in the company, with his hand still extended for an awkward five seconds.

Bob slowly moved his hand to wipe away powder from his sleeve that must have gotten there from one of the donuts. Good recovery, John thought.

As 90 days ticked away, everybody went about their business as usual, doing what they were previously taught, working with their clients and teams within the company. Some actually forgot about the 90-day mark, but not John. He wondered if there would be another department meeting or simply some one-on-one discussions with David.

John was someone who liked things done—a "fixer" of sorts, one who didn't like things unfinished. If it needed to be fixed, he put all his energy into solving the issue. So John, more than others, began to grow anxious during this 90-day period.

Joseph and John had been friends and colleagues since John started. In a way, Joseph helped mentor John in his early days with the company. Joseph was senior-management level and had worn just about every hat in his 23 years at the company. He loved everything about the organization and in fact was a second-generation employee, growing up as a youngster who dreamed of following in his father's footsteps. He had started at the bottom and worked his way up the corporate ladder. This company was all he knew.

David Scares Employees to Motivate

Then, it happened. Joseph received an email to meet in the human resource office at 3:45 p.m. that day, right before most others would be packing up their belongings for the end of their workday.

At 4 p.m. that afternoon, David and a human resource employee informed Joseph that his services were no longer needed, and thanked him for his dedication over the past 23 years. The meeting lasted two minutes. No discussion; no reason given.

David promised to write a great recommendation for Joseph to help him with another job. But what could David possibly write, considering that he knew of Joseph for all of three months.

The next day, a similar situation happened to Jennifer, a 20-year veteran of the company, who did media relations for the organization. Later that day, two more employees found messages from David in their in-boxes. The news spread like wildfire throughout the office. Panic and fear ensued. As employees left the building at the end of the day, they resembled a funeral procession.

As John made his way home to his wife and girls, he was in a state of shock, but relieved that he had survived, at least for that day. He thought, "I gotta get home and get on those unreturned emails. Don't want to give David the impression I'm not a dedicated employee."

As he walked through the door, his girls greeted him with all the love in the world, eager to tell him about their day at school. He tried to pay attention, but his mind was on work.

"I gotta keep my job, keep everyone happy, can't lose the house." All the toxic thoughts running through his mind led him away from the most important thing in his life: his family. How could he have been so blind to David's plan?

Dictator Leadership Only Works for So Long

John and his co-workers worked and lived in fear the next few months: fear for their jobs, for their livelihoods, for their futures. They all worked longer hours, which they believed was better because it was what David clearly wanted. Company production did slightly increase, but their minds were really not on their work. Even worse, their hearts weren't either. They were all in survival mode. They were losing the passion and loyalty that existed prior to David's arrival. John witnessed friendships that had once existed between co-workers now turn sour due to jealousy. People started stealing ideas from others instead of sharing them. It was clear that everyone was out for themselves in the environment David had created. No one was having fun; it was a chore to show up every day.

Over the next three months, production did temporarily improve, yet morale was at an all-time low. David's approach did increase the company's bottom line, due to the salary savings from firing 12 of the 90-plus employees. David never replaced those he fired; instead, an impersonal companywide email simply stated that everyone must "pick up the slack."

John knew this was a toxic environment. His wife and kids felt it too. There was no time for vacations or showing up to the girls' youth basketball games. He even missed their fifth-grade play that they had worked so hard on.

How was this going to get better? Should he look for another job? His anxiety grew as he thought of moving his wife and kids at this pivotal time in their lives.

Then the news came one Friday afternoon. David had taken another job. Another position at a much larger company; more money, more perks, and big-time promotion was the rumor.

And just like that, he was gone. No meeting to tell everyone. No email to say great job to his staff. In fact, as John peered into David's office, he noticed that his desk was already cleared, as if he left in the middle of the night, without a trace.

Short-Term Gain Leads to Long-Term Fixing

John just stood there. He didn't know whether to cry or laugh. Should he be happy, or even more scared? Who would management hire now to pick up the pieces?

As he looked around the office, it reminded him of one of those scenes on the Discovery Channel, when storm chasers film the aftermath of a tornado in a remote town: an immense path of destruction, people in shock, no one knowing what to do.

But John knew that the healing needed to begin. Fix it, he thought. Be a Doer for the company, for his co-workers, and certainly for his girls at home.

Dictator Leadership

Scenarios like these play out every day in many businesses. This dictator leadership has been used since the dawn of time and has been proven to be effective, but only for short-term gains. They don't last and can cause negative outcomes in the long term.

Try this little exercise that helps proves my point. Close your eyes and think of the word dictator, then think of a person in history who resembles what this means to you. Most will think of terrible people like Hitler, Mussolini, Stalin, or Gaddafi.

Perhaps younger folks see someone like Saddam Hussein or Kim Jong-un.

These people ruled through terror and fear. The people around them were scared for their lives. They march, fight, and show fake loyalty out of this fear. But history proves that dictatorships tend to fail in the long term. Most of these brutal self-proclaimed leaders are eventually exiled and even executed. Then the healing process for their nations begins, to rectify the wake of destruction they left behind, which can take years, even decades.

Obviously, we don't exile or execute the dictator executive in the business world. But the story about David illustrates my point about how devastating it can be to lead by fear. People within an organization come to resent these people. Their short-term success is a by-product of the fear they create, and causes destruction to the organization that exists long after they have left.

Dictatorship is *not* sustainable for a company, team, or organization. It is a self-centered style that most people in an organization will quickly sniff out. The long-term damage it causes makes it extremely difficult for the next person who attempts to lead that organization. Long after the dictator departs, employees are left with feelings of mistrust and lack confidence in the next leader. The new supervisor who attempts to right the ship will find it quite difficult to build the trust necessary for a positive work environment. The dictator leader has tarnished the culture, and the healing process takes time. Unfortunately, this becomes a vicious cycle of dictator leaders, because most do not see the value in spending the time to focus on the culture of an organization to build long-term employee success.

Leaders who choose this path in an attempt to grow an organization usually have distinct characteristics. They abuse their authority and lack compassion for others. They tend to be selfish and flex their power often. Employees do not respect this type of leader, and the environment is viewed as corrupt and unfair. Dictator leaders are inclined to make decisions on their own, without considering anyone else's input. These decisions are usually made in the quest for self-promotion, not for the good of the team.

Servant Leadership

I find it interesting when articles come out yearly about the top 10 companies that employees like to work for. Factors include employee satisfaction with leadership, management, and compensation. These companies clearly don't look at quarterly earnings or a single successful sports season, but at long-term growth and development of the organization.

Most of us have gone through change at the leadership level of our school, business, or organization, so we tend to get nervous with organizational leadership change. People want to follow genuine leaders, leaders who encourage, who demonstrate care and respect, and who earn the trust of the employees.

This leads to servant leadership, where the leader with a strong foundation of core values and traits typically is hired. This person is in charge ultimately to serve the organization and will have much more long-term personal and organizational success. Serving your employees takes personal time, energy, money, commitment, and sacrifice. But it leads to an environment that can be positive and productive, and can sustain long-term growth.

Serving your employees does not mean catering to them. There is a clear difference between earning the respect of those you choose to serve and serving just so everyone likes you. Most people will recognize when a leader works hard to earn trust, loyalty, and respect. These leaders create a fair and stable environment, with clear values outlined for everyone to focus on.

A servant leader will work for the good of others, creating an atmosphere where a supervisor will give to each employee. Such leaders demonstrate that they have the backs of everyone within the organization, making sure everyone's needs and priorities are met and focusing on the growth and well-being of everyone on the team. This, in turn, allows employees and team members to feel safe, and work more productively over long periods of time. They become happy with their work and the environment they choose to be in.

Empowerment Leadership

Utilizing servant leadership, combined with the ability to empower people of a group, can be highly successful when building a strong culture. Empowering your team members allows them to take ownership of the organization. When you empower every member of the team, they feel part of the growth process and culture-building procedure.

Some people confuse empowering a team member with an individual promotion within that organization, believing that the only ones to be empowered are those on top. Your team captain, All-American quarterback, best salesperson, or biggest earner in the company tend to be the easy ones to empower, and they take on leadership roles due to their status in a particular group. They are your "superstars."

It is just as important to focus on every member of the team when it comes to empowerment. This is the most critical step not to overlook if you choose to employ empowerment as a leadership style.

> Focus on every member of the team when it comes to empowerment.

It is the players who are not starters or first-year hires that you need to be involved with and spend much of your time as the leader of the organization. Find ways to empower these people. The more time you invest in these folks, the more they begin to trust you and become loyal. Their production might not be at superstar status yet, but your job in the mentoring process is essential to the long-term growth of these individuals and the organization as a whole. Ask the rookie employee to sit in on a big sales meeting. Spend quality one-on-one time mentoring the person in charge of cleaning up the office after everyone has left for the day. It takes a commitment from the leader to serve and empower everyone.

This commitment plays a vital part in servant leadership. It builds the trust needed between a player and a coach, or an administrator and an employee. Giving those around you the ability to grow, learn, fail, and persevere through your leadership mentoring will lead to huge advances for them.

> When you serve and empower as a leader, you allow employees to see just how much they are valued.

When you serve and empower as a leader, you allow employees to see just how much they are valued. Remember, it is your daily role to invest in the mentoring process as you build leaders. Understand that there will be setbacks, failures, and even resistance. Stick to the core values you believe in; the culture you create will have others follow your lead. Realize that not everyone will grow to superstar status. Yet if you can grow each person 5% each week, you have the ability to create an environment that will eventually produce a few superstars. This, in turn, allows you to become a servant leader. We will address the 5% rule in Chapter 16, and I am convinced no organization can achieve growth and long-term success without the leader believing in it.

Relying on Both Forms of Leadership

Keep in mind that servant and empowerment leadership can stand alone or be intertwined. What works best really depends on everchanging factors. It could be what works best for you as the leader. Or, because employees constantly change, a leader may need to adjust teaching styles to best fit each employee. Upper management changes and their ideas of leadership could have a trickle-down effect, forcing a quality leader into a role they are not comfortable with.

Most likely, you will find it best to have both forms of positive leadership in your portfolio of leadership styles, as they can both be beneficial when building a positive culture within your organization.

Most successful people don't want a "nice" boss. They want a respectful, fair, and loyal leader. That's what motivates the people you need to surround yourself with to produce a positive, productive, and successful organization.

Coach's Challenge

1. How can you employ a few tactics to better serve the people around you within your workplace?
2. Who on your team can you empower who doesn't quite have the status or leadership roles of your "superstars" or "captains"?

3. Do you, as a leader, look around and take the necessary steps to care for everyone around you?

4. Can you find ways for those you have served to demonstrate growth? Become healthier? Wiser?

5. Ultimately, can you find others you have served now serving others?

7

Are You a Brick with Mortar?

When you read about a successful NFL coach or watch an interview after championships are won, you hear words like "toughness," "blue collar," and "gritty." This is often how leaders describe their teams' reactions when the chips are on the line. When it comes to building a strong culture for your program or organization, leaders want those "grinders" around them. We think they'll be the hardest-working, most reliable, and best able to get though the muck that will be dealt to a group over a period of time.

But what is real "toughness?" What does grit mean when describing a person within your organization?

Imagine a weekly staff meeting at a huge firm, where the account supervisor announces, "I want to point out how proud we all are of Julie's efforts this past month. She sealed one of our biggest contracts to date with a client we have been chasing for months. She showed determination and grit, going the extra mile with late hours and weekends to accomplish this account. Let's give her a big round of applause!"

What did the supervisor mean by grit? What is true toughness? I frequently ask these questions of people who have built championship programs or successful businesses.

True Toughness

A prevalent answer is that toughness is not a value or trait; it is a combination of many ideas, values, and traits that each individual in the organization is willing to invest in.

> Toughness is a combination of many ideas,
> values, and traits that each individual in
> the organization is willing to invest in.

Being tough is not about how loud you are or how much you posture to intimidate others. Toughness is commonly misunderstood to equate to fist fights and verbal arguments. I call it the "hold me back" theory: the person who is posturing how "tough" they think they are by picking a fight or engaging in a shouting match. I chuckle every fall when I turn on a college football game, especially during rivalry week, when teams play longstanding foes. As the two teams come together for pregame warmups at the 50-yard line, they begin to yell and scream at each other. At first glance it looks to be a battle royal or rumble about to go down, a true street fight. Everyone is telling their teammates "Hold me back!" This is fake toughness, just like the two guys in a bar arguing over who bumped whom in the line to get a drink. One tells a friend, "Hold me back before I beat the pulp out of this guy!"

I always wonder what would happen if the person who is supposedly holding them back lets them go. Those college players surely know the NCAA or the schools they play for would hand down hefty suspensions or rip their eligibility away, costing them not only issues with their scholarships, but potentially their professional careers! The bouncer in that bar would quickly throw those two fellas on the street or even have them arrested. All these situations are fake toughness—just talk.

> If you want to be tough, follow your core values.

Real toughness is an individual who is willing to follow a set of standards put forth by the leader of a program or organization in order to do their part for the greater good of that organization.

People who demonstrate grit stick to these principles, even when faced with a setback, failure, or adversity. When a group of people follow this pattern, the program becomes tough, resilient, tenacious. All these values and traits we strive for allow us to form a strong culture. So if you want to be tough, follow your core values.

Learn to Compete

Have a great attitude and stay positive when things don't necessarily go the way you planned. Learn how to compete in everything you engage in. Challenge yourself and you're co-workers to compete every day. Competition tests your true toughness.

Your compete level will help you prepare for the everyday challenges that will arise on playing fields and in boardrooms. And it *has* to be practiced. Set up daily plans to compete with one another. There is a huge difference during competition between having fun and doing something rewarding. Everyone wants to have fun, but only few substitute it for something rewarding. That is another sign of toughness.

Toughness is also brought out through competition simply because competition will ultimately lead to winners and losers, or success and failure. During the tough times of losing, setbacks, and failure, your toughness will be tested. The end result that comes from competing drives an individual to relate back to the core values their organization established. If you beat out your co-worker for a promotion, show humility toward them to help them grow. If you lose your starting position on a sports team, recognize the value of failure as a positive teaching tool in order to improve tomorrow. When competition exists both within an organization and against opponents, the outcome will always test your core values. When you have an opportunity to demonstrate these values, it gives you the opportunity to show true toughness.

Competing has to be practiced.

I see this every day when recruiting Division I baseball players to our program. There has been a cultural change in our sport, like others. It used to be that winning a game or championship at the high school level meant more than individual success. Unfortunately, we have entered the "travel ball" era. Now, not all travel ball organizations operate as I am about to describe and actually engage in a team concept, but the majority have set the tone of individual as oppose to organizational success. Players don't necessarily represent a town or high school team anymore, but they play for a team consisting of players from all over a region or even a state, that they pay exorbitant fees to be a part of in order to play in front of college and professional scouts. People like me, scouting for future talent, are forced to attend these games, as most parents buy into the pressure to have their sons or daughters play in order to obtain scholarships. What is not explained is that scholarships are very rare, and with tens of thousands of players around the country, a participant really has to stand out. What transpires at these travel games is athletes playing to impress scouts, not to win the game. In fact, some games have time limits and no one even knows the score.

Also, players on the travel teams who don't like a coach or get benched for not hustling just leave and take their payment to another organization. The competition necessary for these young players to be successful in baseball and later in life is lacking. These games are for individual rewards, and not for the reward of a team championship. A strong group culture rarely forms from this model.

Let's switch gears for a moment, out of the sports world, and paint a picture of the travel ball mentality in the corporate world. Can you envision paying a sum of money to a business you would like to work for? Imagine that you have to pay them to work, in exchange for many larger rewards, such as higher pay and better jobs once you leave this company.

All the people inside that office building also pay to be there. So your colleagues consist of employees who "pay to play." They come from all over the United States to join this organization. The supervisor of this group gets everyone together, most likely once a month, and asks everyone to demonstrate their skills in order to win a huge account. There are no internal meetings, no training sessions, no discussions on how to win the big account, and certainly no time that everyone on the team spends together. No team bond has time to form.

Everyone is on their own and employees are asked to add to the overall success of winning this particular account. Yet there is one caveat in this office: everyone will work for individual rewards. If you perform, you get the bonus, not the others on your team or within the group. If you stand out among your peers, you win, not the team.

In this scenario, there certainly will be great internal competition, which as we discussed is vital in the early stages when building a program. Yet this internal competition will not back down once the group is after the same carrot, or account. What ensues is a ton of friction within the organization, which certainly will derail the long-term success of this group.

This is what I see when recruiting young adults from travel ball teams. As their potential future coach, I must take the time and energy to unravel this mentality in order to build the culture we feel is vital for the long-term success of our program.

It becomes more difficult to find young players who love the competition to win as a team, as opposed to the individual glory and success.

Bricks and Mortar

Whether I work with my own program or speak to an organization on building leadership, I ask them if they can envision themselves as a brick in their organization and think about what that means. They tell me a brick is tough, hard, and a foundation of the program. Bricks stand the test of time. They weather well and don't crumble easily. In groups, they can be hard to move. If you had a choice of being in a brick structure or a wooden one during a hurricane, naturally you would choose the brick one for safety. So most people want to be labeled a brick in an organization.

I do an exercise where I pass out an individual brick to each of them and ask them to make it their own by writing their name on it. Next, I ask them to go to a table positioned in the front of the room and place their brick either on top of or beside another brick. More times than not, the group stacks their bricks to form a mini wall. I then scan the room and usually find some form of a cinderblock or brick wall within eyesight; if not, I tell them to visualize one close by. As I approach the group's stack of bricks, I explain how everyone has the capabilities to be just like the brick with their name on it. And with one simple push, I topple the bricks as if they were made of foam.

By themselves, bricks hold some weight and capabilities, but without other bricks, they can't accomplish much. And more important, what holds them together through the storm? Well, that's the mortar—the gritty substance made of a sticky, sandy, moist material. It holds each brick together with a strong bond. Without mortar, bricks can topple with ease. The wall of bricks may look strong, but without mortar it doesn't have the strength or toughness it appears to have. So even though people in an organization view themselves as bricks, more is needed to make them truly strong.

> Mortar establishes the culture of one's organization.

What makes the "mortar" within an organization?

I explain this as the formation of core values the team must engage in. This mortar establishes the culture of one's organization. It consistently acts as a bonding agent to hold all the organizational bricks together, allowing the entire wall to stand tall and tough for many years to come.

Values are what the leader presents to the team to follow, especially during tough times. That is when true toughness and grit is put to the test. It is easy to be a leader, or a brick, when times are good. But how do you get out of slumps, or turn around poor quarterly earnings? You revert back to your values that define your successful program. Throughout this book, we navigate through values and traits a leader not only needs to have, but must instill in the individuals within the organization to find true, long-term success.

> You must set a positive environment, with a stable group of core values, in order to create a winning culture.

Many times we hear of great organizations and teams that have unbelievable talent, yet fail to succeed. A pro team obtains high-level all-star players through free agency and trades, hoping to assemble a roster of the best players. Or a CEO sways top executives and a sales force from other companies to assemble a corporate sales "dream team." The person in charge recruits really good bricks. Yet when these superstars in their respected fields join together without core values and a strong culture, it can be quite difficult to succeed. Although you, as a leader, need the competition and egos that go with high-level performers, you must create a positive environment, with a stable group of core values, in order to create a "winning" culture.

So, as a leader, you need to find bricks, to surround yourself with the good people you think have the capabilities to succeed in the environment and culture you are working hard to achieve. Then it is your responsibility to mix the mortar. Find the values you want your people to strive for. Remember the value wall at Stetson? Come up with your organization's own set of values. Remember not to overload your bricks with too many ideas. Constantly work your values into the culture you want to create. There will certainly be setbacks and naysayers; that is part of the growth process. Not only will these setbacks and failures happen, but they are necessary for you and your organization to grow for long-term success.

Learn to "Pivot" with Your Mortar

A common mistake many leaders make is that once they feel they have established a strong list of core values, and build a positive and productive culture, they believe that culture will always exist.

Quite the contrary—there are many moving parts and puzzle pieces to any organization or team. People will leave for other jobs, or even transition within the same organization into a different role. Technology is ever changing, requiring employees to become educated with new ideas and products. Team members can become complacent when success happens, believing it only gets easier to obtain with time. This couldn't be further from the truth; it is difficult enough to be successful, let alone sustain long-term success.

Due to these factors that can derail the culture of an organization, everyone must be willing to change as situations change. You, as their leader, need to be on the constant lookout for culture changes that could adversely affect the organization. When recognized, either pivot the group to new ways to engage in core values, or remind them of what brought past successes.

> Once you have good mortar, those bricks
> will certainly stick together and be strong
> as the test of time.

Again, think of your values as that mortar that holds your bricks, or employees, together. What happens when mortar sits outside in the sun too long? It dries out. What if you add too much water to the mortar? It becomes runny and won't stick to any bricks. When mortar is too watery, you add grit; too dry, you add liquid.

In the corporate world this needs to happen to sustain long-term success. If you or your organization are dealt adversity, get a little tougher and revert to the core values everyone set. Become more positively assertive with one another to foster competition within your team, driving everyone to be better prepared for competition against opponents. Or maybe you have to back off a little and allow people some space to live through their values. Once you pay constant attention to these values, your "organizational mortar" can change to the consistency needed to make it work. It bonds the people of an organization—the bricks—tighter and makes it tougher to bring them down.

At times, it seems a bit of a puzzle to fix your mortar. Some combinations of the mixing process work, and some don't. Your mortar can even start out perfect but may need to be addressed after some time. Yet once you have good mortar, those bricks will certainly stick together and be strong enough to stand the test of time.

So, we can have tough people, which is essential to a strong culture. Yet, the true grit of the organization is infusing the people (the bricks) with a set of important values (the mortar). Be a strong leader who can find good people for the organization or team, then invest as much energy as you possibly can in the values and culture you feel is best. Your mortar will constantly change, so make sure you pay attention to these foreseeable revisions that will need to be addressed. It will pay dividends when you define the success of your organization.

Coach's Challenge

1. What values do you believe can lead to someone being "tough"?
2. What are some traits that demonstrate a person who possesses true grit?
3. What challenges have you faced when trying to bond your bricks together?
4. How do you utilize setbacks and failures to strengthen your mortar and brick wall?

8

The Value of Real Energy

After a big win, we often hear the coach talking about the energy their team possessed. Or the CEO of a successful organization speaks of the great intensity and vigor the employees put forth in order to make the quarterly earnings report to shareholders the best in its the company's history.

"The energy in the clubhouse was electric tonight!" a coach or player might say. "Our sales team put together a proposal that will surely land the account we've been after for six months now. I appreciate the energy they put into this effort!" a supervisor announces to the company.

Yet what is energy? Is it science? A cosmic force that we cannot explain?

Energy is one of those words that have multiple definitions. It could apply to an active person, or to usable power, such as a heating source. When a group leader uses the term to describe a positive trait with an organization or team, it's typically to commend everyone for their effort when accomplishing a task or goal. But I find myself asking, "What is *real* energy?"

In my opinion, the word energy is overused. I constantly hear coaches and business leaders use it, and it appears in books and movies and on advertisement billboards. Yet the people using this term often don't have the slightest clue what it means to have it!

We previously discussed real versus fake toughness and the posturing that athletes sometimes do in order to intimidate their opponents, like the "hold me back" scenario on the 50-yard line at the college football game. I see similarities to that fake toughness when considering fake versus real energy.

Real versus Fake Energy

Fake energy can also be seen as "nervous" energy, such as when a person tries to show everyone how hard they're working, or when a person tries to overcorrect in order to show they know what they're talking about. These people try to flex their dominant personality to impress and motivate others within the organization. Someone with fake energy tends to overprepare and underperform, being unable to calmly handle adversity or invoke crisis-management skills.

In my first few years of coaching at the Division I level, I worked with a colleague who coached another sport in my athletic department and was thought to be a little crazy and out of control. He was the type of person that couldn't sit through a staff meeting, and when he did, he fidgeted or doodled on scrap paper. He talked so fast, it was hard to follow what he was saying. He coached the same way—1,000 miles an hour. I believed he was a bit out of control, in coaching and in his everyday life, but he believed this was what constitutes hard work. He sold himself on outworking everyone and had more energy than his coaching peers. In fact, one day he proclaimed to a group of us that he made coffee nervous.

Yet I always wondered, was he working harder than everyone else? Or was he just wasting time, and energy trying to prove to everyone how hard he was working?

> Before you can lead with your voice, you
> must lead by your actions.

More often than not, employees see right through someone who displays fake energy. Most will recognize the false work ethic and see that this person is not genuine in the energy they are so desperate to exhibit. Ironically, this type of individual tends to burn out quickly. I believe the fake and nervous energy burns through the "stored calories" of real effort and energy, and thus only short-term success is achieved.

Conversely, genuine, sincere energy actually comes from sticking to the principles and values one recognizes as a priority. That is, when a person can focus on a few important values they deem critical, and stick to them with a positive attitude, this demonstrates real energy.

A true leader will be consistent in following the organization's values, sharing ideas and constantly encouraging others to strive forward. They invoke a servant leadership model, and empower others within the group to take risks, learn from their mistakes, and grow. They are the ultimate optimists and they do what they say they will do. They understand what it means to be a grinder and work in a blue-collar way. Yet they don't feel the need to advertise it; rather, they show their value to the group by their actions.

When you possess real energy and demonstrate with actions, this is a vital step in becoming a leader. You let your body of work speak for itself, instead of telling everyone within your group how to do it. When someone talks about how hard they work, or shows off fake energy, it does not speak the volumes one might think it does. Before you can lead with your voice, you must lead by your actions. Real energy can naturally display your positive attitude and core values, because your positivity and attention to these values will clearly demonstrate your dedication. A person with real energy does what they say they will do and doesn't just tell everyone how they will do it.

They focus on the core values the team sets and have a vision just how to stick to them as an individual and with the group. They are willing to take chances and understand that sometimes they will fail.

> A person with real energy does what they say they will do and doesn't just tell everyone how they will do it.

True energy people tend to be persistent, stubborn, and high achievers. They don't use excuses or blame luck when it doesn't go their way. They plug away and never give in or give up. They become "doers," not "sayers."

Don't Give Up and Don't Be a Lake

It is vital to have real energy to be persistent and consistent. Real energy people will not take no for an answer or fuel themselves from any doubt or negativity from others. They stick to their principles and keep their emotions in check. They know that a roller coaster ride of emotions and constantly changing their principles won't lead to success.

> Real energy people stick to their principles and keep their emotions in check.

If you've been around a mountainous setting with a climate that produces snow, or live in the great state of Maine, you know what happens each spring. Melting snow causes an immense amount of water to infiltrate lakes, fields, roadways, and lawns. Native "Mainahs" don't call it spring—it's mud season. Everywhere you go, mud exists. Many lakes and rivers in this region rise so high, they overflow, causing even more mud!

Genuine energy people don't let emotions, attitude, or effort go up and down, like the lakes in mud season throughout Maine. They know how to keep negativity and pessimism from affecting their values.

One particular player I coached was named Ian, who walked onto our team, meaning that he didn't earn a scholarship with our program. But he decided to try out for the last remaining spot on the roster, a spot usually reserved for one of the 30 or so students who wanted to try out for this last position on the team. Ian was from Brooklyn, and was very physical in stature but lacked other skills necessary to be a complete Division I player. He could hit, but defense wasn't his strong suit. In fact, his arm strength was one of the weakest I've coached at this level of baseball.

Yet Ian had heart and an infallible desire to make the roster that year. He worked out by himself, even when he thought no one was watching. In my observation, he was a genuine "doer" not someone trying to show off, but instead leading by action.

So when it came time to make cuts to our roster, I decided Ian would fill our last remaining spot. I told him there were no promises, and he most likely would not even travel with the team that season. I laid out what I thought he needed to improve on, and told him I would work with him as my time permitted.

Ian was persistent and used my evaluation as his motivation. Most people say they have been in this type of situation before, but Ian really did it. He grinded out each and every team workout and improved. Ian proved, not only to himself but to me and the entire team as well, that he could have an impact if called upon during a game situation. He wasn't a "lake" going through ups and downs filled with excuses and emotions.

A week before our first game, at UNLV in Las Vegas, I posted the travel roster, and I made the decision not to take Ian on this trip, leaving him off the list. I told him that although he worked hard, there were a few other players I thought were better at the time to help the team win.

Ian didn't roll his eyes in disgust, slam his fist in frustration, or sulk. Instead, he looked me in the eye and said, "Coach, I got it. You make the decisions best for the team. I will be ready when you ask for me."

His calm, confident voice made me think that he really believed what he said. He didn't just say those words; he meant it. He had a positive attitude in what was a negative situation for him and showed me what I knew was great energy.

Two days later, another freshman on the team who played the same position as Ian decided to head downtown and take liberties at a local watering hole. Being a freshman, he was under age to be in this establishment. As a result of his indiscretions, he was handed down a four-game suspension that opened up a travel spot the night before we were scheduled to leave for Las Vegas.

I called Ian about 9 p.m. that night and told him to pack his bags because I had decided to take him on the trip. I was expecting him to be emotional, or at least a bit excited.

But Ian just said calmly, "Okay, I'll be ready."

As the opening weekend went on, and we engaged in a four-game series with UNLV, I didn't play Ian. It wasn't until game three that I looked down the dugout bench in the later innings and saw Ian with his batting helmet and gloves on, bat in hand. He was ready for an at-bat, if I chose to put him in. I decided to call his name and let him hit. Again, Ian showed no emotion, but was focused with real, genuine energy.

He hit a double in his first collegiate at-bat.

The next day, in the final game of the series, I decided to start him. He went 3–4 with 2 doubles at the plate.

Ian never came out of the starting lineup for four years, and earned All-American honors his first year. Today, Ian works in New York City, running a business and continues to "grind" it out, with real energy, better than most. Ian was not a lake during Maine's mud season. He stayed full, because he had real energy, with a positive attitude.

Optimistic or Embellishment?

Being a leader can be quite difficult, especially when you're in a negative environment or around pessimistic people. Staying positive in gloomy situations at the workplace or in everyday life is an essential characteristic of the best leaders. I believe it's the very toughest thing to do when you navigate the challenges leadership brings.

Every day, I try to bring a positive attitude that reflects my definition of real energy. I hope my attitude will be contagious and rub off on those around me, whether players, fellow coaches, or co-workers. I believe my energy can "energize" others.

However, I've noticed something when it comes to real energy and having an optimistic approach to daily challenges. Some may believe you are not optimistic at all, but rather one who embellishes, inflates, or exaggerates. You become labeled a "bullshitter" or a "used car salesman." These negative Nellies don't view you as someone who always looks for the good in a situation—the glass half full. They are fueled by jealousy and negativity, wanting you to fail. Unfortunately, their pessimistic views differ from your overly optimistic approach, which drives them to think you embellish.

This is something that happens to me all the time. I think of my situation a few years ago as Division I college baseball coach at UMaine. Mind you, the college baseball season is played February till late May—not the best weather to be outside at one of the northernmost universities in the country.

My takeaway was always this: what a great opportunity to travel, see other places, and bond as a team. Also, how many of our opponents are tough enough to travel for three months straight, not playing a home game for the first 30 contests on the schedule. We had an opportunity to prove we were tougher than everybody else!

I can say I truly believed this, and had no room to surround myself with others who didn't see the opportunity we had, as opposed to the negative backlash that someone might think. Looking back now from my Florida office overlooking the stadium one 70-degree December day, I wondered, "What was I thinking!?" Yet I believed there was good to come from a not-so-good situation. You just need to know how to dig deep and find it.

I can assure you, those who will call you an embellisher just don't have the ability to have real energy or possess a positive outlook when dealt difficult situations. In fact, a major factor is jealousy. The negative Nellies who rain on your parade really are jealous that they don't possess the ability to be like you! Their name calling and negativity is their defense mechanism to cover their own poor attitude.

Although people use the word energy in many ways to describe a person, it has defining personality traits. Those who have the ability to show real energy are the ultimate optimists. They have a positive outlook in every situation, no matter how good or bad. Their true toughness is their ability to follow core values they set, allowing them to give off a vibe of infectious energy.

Although "energy" can be used in many ways to describe a person, it clearly has defining traits that are present in one's personality and can help those possessing it to become stronger leaders.

Coach's Challenge

1. What values or traits do you possess that help give you real energy?

2. Have you ever been called an embellisher? Did you see a negative Nellie in that person?

3. How can you avoid becoming a lake in Maine during mud season?

4. Give an example where you led your group by your actions before you led by your voice.

9

Good Impressions

Have you ever found yourself gravitating toward a certain product when purchasing goods? Or not even checking the prices in front of the gas station, just pulling into the lot of the same name-brand company each time you need gasoline? Or sticking with good ol' Chevy (or Ford) when shopping for a pickup truck?

Companies like Coke versus Pepsi or UPS versus FedEx infiltrate college campuses and offer lucrative deals to obtain exclusivity rights to sell their products, in hopes of these college graduates growing into executive leaders one day and making decisions on what companies to use when running a business for their products. It's all about image and brand recognition.

In my position as a college baseball coach, it is vital to recruit quality student athletes to be a part of our program. I am going to be around these 18- to 22-year-olds nonstop for the next four years and not only do I need good players with high athletic skills, but there is so much more expected of the recruit. They represent me, the school, the former players, and all the alums of the university.

"Surround Yourself with Good People"

My college coach, legendary Division III Baseball Hall of Fame Coach Bill Holowaty, was a master of repeating phrases and routines that had significant meaning to him. His motto was "Surround yourself with good people, and good things will happen. Surround yourself with bad people, and you will be in bad situations much of the time."

So what constitutes a good person?

That is certainly a matter of opinion, depending on what traits you, as a leader, value in others. We've already discussed some of these values. But having good people surrounding your organization or team also relates to another important value: image.

Image is the reason you make many—perhaps most—of your daily choices and decisions. You choose certain products and even friendships or partnerships based on image. There are so many good products out there, yet more times than not, you're actually buying the person selling you the product, not the product itself, because you fell in love with the image they created, not necessarily the product they are selling.

Let's use the paper industry for our example of how image has great purchasing power. Say you work in an office where your role is to purchase office supplies for the entire organization. Salespeople from competing paper companies are constantly looking to supply your office with copy paper. One salesperson stops by, gives his pitch and pricing and leaves, hoping for your business.

The next salesperson takes her time with you to invest in genuine conversation and build a relationship. She leaves that first meeting without asking for your business, but wanting to come back the following week. Upon her return, she brings you a gift, a book about the best hikes in Vermont and also asks how your daughters' soccer game from the past weekend turn out. How did she know you like to hike in Vermont or have a kid who plays soccer? Ah, yes, you discussed these things in the previous week's meeting. People like this make you feel comfortable and you like the image they personally set.

Now, paper is paper and there really is no difference from one sheet to the next when purchasing office paper. Salesperson 2 might even charge slightly more. But who are you going to sign a paper contract with? Most likely the one who created a relationship, through image, to get you to believe theirs is the best choice.

Be on the Lookout for Values

When I recruit potential student athletes, the easy part is seeing who actually has the skills to play at the highest levels. A radar gun can tell me if they have the arm strength to throw 90-mph fastballs, or I can see someone hit a 400-foot home run. Similarly, when evaluating a new hire to join your organization you can clearly see their college degree, GPA, and list of accomplishments. Yet, does the fancy degree or the athletic talent guarantee this person is a good addition to your team?

What makes a strong hire or a good recruit for a college baseball team are not necessarily the splashy words on a resume or how far you can hit the ball but the core values you can find within each person.

Now, don't get me wrong. I have said you need strong horses to win the race, meaning you do need to have the tools and skills in place to be successful in your field. Yet, the complete "superstar" has those other qualities that are not measured in a quantitative way. Rather, these individuals possess traits and values that clearly set them apart from the rest.

Part of the recruiting process of college baseball is not only watching players perform and finding out who has the skills to be successful, but getting to know these student athletes. Are they coachable?

The same holds true for business leaders seeking employees. Once you've narrowed down the stack of resumes for a critical opening in your organization, you most likely engage in either phone or Skype interviews to evaluate the person, "in person." You want to know how they present themselves, what their conversational style is, and whether you can see yourself working alongside this person on a daily basis.

You are looking for the value of image the potential hire presents. And the applicant usually has only about 30 seconds to make a lasting impression in the interview.

After I watch a potential baseball recruit, I then dive into finding out as much as I can. And, unfortunately, you can't always believe what you hear. In fact, in my business, travel ball coaches are paid largely to "sell" their players to collegiate programs. It is difficult to get a true grasp of someone when the recommendation is coming from a person being paid to give a good recommendation! Another situation where you can't believe what you hear is when the applicant may be on the chopping block in their current role. When you call for a verbal recommendation you may get a false sense of this individual, simply based on the fact that their current employer wishes this person to move on to another job. Pass the buck!

> A true test of one's character is how hard they are willing to work when no one is watching.

When recruiting potential student athletes, I take the painstaking time to research the individual to gather valuable information before inviting them to join us. I go back and watch a player when they don't know I'm there and observe how they react when they think no one is there to see them play. Do they throw their helmet when they strike out? Does the hustle only exist when a college coach is present? I constantly remind myself of a saying another hall of fame coach I played for, Rick Jones, used to say every day: "A true test of one's character is how hard they are willing to work when no one is watching."

I continually look for this value in people, the image they will present if they join our organization. Any potential additions to our program will represent me, our team, our entire university, former players, and alumni. So, make sure you do your homework and look for underlying values, like image, and don't fall in love with the talent alone that potential recruits demonstrate at first glance.

Learn from Communicating

Of course, the best way to get a handle on a person is communication. Strong communication is key to the recruiting and hiring process. With the advent of e-mail, texting, Twitter, Facebook, and other social media, communication approaches have certainly changed in recent years. But there is absolutely no substitute for a good old face-to-face conversation. As we discussed earlier, there is tremendous value in an in-person meeting, which allows you to see nonverbal cues such as gestures, facial expressions, and body language.

Because investing in people is critical to the success of my team, I utilize many forms of communication. One example of investing in the college athletic arena is scholarship dollars, and comparable in the business world to compensation dollars. So, whether you're investing in players or employees, careful consideration is critical and costly to the bottom line. The appearance and talent that a potential employee or athlete possesses is just the first step in the hiring process. Remember, as a leader, you are going to hang your hat on both this person's performance and the image they bring to your organization. They represent you, your team, and the entire organization as a whole. Take time to seek out the values in people before bringing them on board. Resist love at first sight until you evaluate the whole person; don't simply base your decision on the 400-foot home run or the terrific resume highlights.

30 Seconds

In most situations, 30 seconds is all you have to make a lasting impression. Anyone who has ever worked recruiting in college sports knows what it's like to watch six baseball games, sunup to midnight, for a week-long tourney. But it is necessary to make the huge investment of a full scholarship in a future player for the team. This parallels the salary, commissions, and bonuses you are potentially offering a recruit to join your business. These lucrative offers are tools to entice the individual to join your organization. You've already identified their talents, skills, and knowledge in the hope of mentoring them as members of your organization.

Let me paint a picture of something that happens quite often. After I get back from a week on the road of recruiting, watching many travel ballgames, I collect a list of players' names. Back in my office, I call the top names on the list. First up is Billy, who's big, strong, fast, and hustles. He demonstrated a great work ethic and he was a positive team player. Whether he hit a home run or struck out, his demeanor and attitude were the same: professional and positive.

As often happens today with young millennials, the call goes straight to voice mail. After listening to his polite outgoing message, I leave mine: "Hey Billy, this is Steve Trimper, the head baseball coach at Stetson University. I had a chance to watch you play this week and was impressed with not only your performance, but also with your hustle and competitiveness. I would like to speak to you about visiting our university, and about the opportunity to earn a baseball scholarship as a student athlete."

Next up is Michael. Michael is another strong and talented player but with a host of negative behaviors: arrogance, pretension, and conceit. He showed too much cockiness as he jogged out a fly ball, instead of the hustle I was looking for. He rolled his eyes when an umpire called a strike. But if I can get him on our team, maybe I can mentor him, and get him to tone this down once he's around the good people we've already asked to join our program.

Once again, I pick up the phone, prepared for another voice-mail. Except this experience is far different, Michael's outgoing message is littered with expletives, backed by loud music.

My reaction is bewilderment. Think about that: an athlete losing out on a $250k investment because of that experience in the first 30 seconds. Michael might actually be a good individual, yet my decision to invest in him has severely diminished.

The image you create in those critical first 30 seconds of meeting someone usually sticks.

"Recruit Ready"

We can all recall a particular instance, event, or impactful day that brought meaning to our lives. For me, it was the first day on the job at Stetson University as their new head baseball coach. My hiring was actually quite a unique situation. Most collegiate baseball coaching changes happen in June, at the end of the season. However, in 2016, long-time head baseball coach Pete Dunn, the legendary coach at Stetson for the previous 38 years, decided it was time to step down and retire just prior to Christmas. So, there I was, freezing my butt off in early December at the University of Maine, and a few short weeks later I found myself in DeLand, Florida, as Stetson's new coach. My wife stayed behind in Maine for a few months preparing for the big move while I hit the ground running in Florida. It was already Christmas season, but it felt like Christmas morning every day because I was so excited that first month. I was now in charge of a top baseball program in Division I, and the weather was awesome after those winters in Maine! With no place to live in the short term, I appreciated that the university was generous enough to put me up in a hotel close to campus for the first month as I searched for a more permanent place to live.

My move to Florida happened to be when all the students were on winter break, so I had to wait a few weeks to meet my new team. My excitement certainly kept me from sleeping in; I wanted to invest as much time as I could on campus those first few weeks. I had a routine of getting an early start, and taking a jog around the campus as the sun was rising. Each day I was amazed to see a stir around campus at such an early hour. Leaf blowers, lawn mowers, and Weedwackers were roaring. Workers hustled around sweeping sidewalks and cleaning glass entry doors. Every day I witnessed this busy bee mentality, even, to my surprise, on Saturdays and Sundays!

If you've ever been to Stetson's campus, you know how beautiful it is. Palms and oaks adorn the grounds, draped with Spanish moss hanging so low you can touch it. The grass is so perfectly cut it makes you wonder if it's real. It's truly a lovely setting to attend school.

After a few weeks of my early morning routine, I asked the athletic director's assistant, Stacy, what the deal was with all the workers. Stacy explained that when the current president, Wendy B. Libby, PhD, arrived at the university seven years earlier, the campus was in not great shape. Her first order of business, rather than increasing the faculty of the already reputable university, was to find the budget to hire a horde of grounds crew. I have since gotten to know Wendy and her husband, Richard, quite well, as they are huge supporters of many of the clubs and teams at Stetson. She is not only extremely intelligent, but she is also a savvy businesswoman. In fact, during her tenure as president, she has grown Stetson tenfold, with modern buildings, new academic majors, and a growing capital endowment fund that the board of trustees could only have dreamt of when they appointed her. Being ranked one of the top academic schools in the South was very important to her, but she also valued the ranking of the top schools in the region as a beautiful campus.

After a few weeks, I finally got the chance to spend some time with Dr Libby. During one of our conversations, I told her about my early morning runs and how impressed I was with the campus and its appearance.

"Recruit-ready, Steve," she responded. "We need to have our campus ready at any moment to impress a future student, potential employee, or athlete."

We only get one chance at a first impression.

She wanted the place in tip-top shape before the workday began. I was really impressed by her desire to create a positive image of Stetson, and valued her passion. To this day, I find myself constantly pitching in to make Stetson "recruit-ready." If I see trash on the ground, I pick it up. I watch others do the same. Everyone on campus, including the students, help make the place beautiful. Dr. Libby's creation of image not only benefits the potential for future growth, but she has created an environment that is contagious. Just like the infectious attitude we discussed earlier, image can also be mimicked by others within an organization.

The impact you can have, as a member of any company or team, is immense.

This is why promotions, personal advancements, and bonuses exist: supervisors see the value in the image you bring to the company. And leaders want to reward their people for employees not only doing their part, but going above the call of their job titles.

You Need a Personality

I once spoke to a group of bankers at their annual corporate retreat. The bank president in the town I was coaching at was a corporate sponsor of the university. He told me the bank was struggling with motivating employees and with getting the profit numbers up. He asked me to spend a few hours sharing ideas on leadership and team building, to help them understand how important they considered each member of the organization to be.

Interestingly, a week prior to this presentation, I was in a rush to get my twin daughters to hockey practice and I needed to cash the $10 check my 87-year-old grandmother sends every year for my birthday. (I have tried to rip it up in the past, but I get the wrath of her anger if I don't cash it.) I just happened to be driving by this particular bank at the time, and although I didn't have an account with them, I decided to see if they could help me.

At the drive-up window, a young teller with a huge smile and bubbly personality told me she could certainly help me cash the check. After a few minutes, she sent a $10 bill through the teller drawer. I thanked her for saving me time. "No problem Mr. Trimper, I'm happy to help. Have a great day! Oh, and happy birthday. You look great for turning 29 today!" (It was actually my 45th birthday.) From the back seat of my truck, my twin daughters were quick to remind me of my real age. "Dad, you're not 29, you're just old!"

How did she know it was my birthday? I had handed her my driver's license to cash the check, and she took the time not only to recognize my date of birth, but make a little joke about how young I looked!

I turned to my daughters. "Girls, I apologize, but we're going to be late to practice today." I pulled my truck into a parking spot and went into the bank to meet up with the lead teller to open a new account.

Fast-forward to the presentation the president of this same bank asked me to make. I hoped my talk would help get everyone on the same page, and I shared my thoughts on the values of attitude, image, energy, and so on. But the teller's actions the week prior gave me some great material to speak about the impact of someone's actions. I shared the check-cashing birthday story with the entire group, and how this particular teller's image and attitude led me to take the time to switch business to her company. In fact, I continue to bank with them today, even after I moved out of the state. It was great to call her out and she actually stood up in the crowd of 400 tellers to be recognized. She certainly deserved it.

What this teller demonstrated is another key factor that aids the image you create: she had a personality.

> To be successful, it takes a personality that is infectious in a positive and genuine way.

She clearly liked her job. She valued the quick interaction with me and invested in it. Being able to surround yourself with people who have good personalities is key—they are the backbone of a solid and successful organization.

The image you choose to put forth in those impactful first 30 seconds can have lasting effects, and can make or break your involvement with a team, organization, or business. Image, conversely, is hard to change. A negative first impression can linger and can be difficult to recover from. It is equally important for leaders to model positive self-image. After all, you never know who is evaluating.

Coach's Challenge

1. List your core values that you look for in a "good person" for your team.

2. What are some ways to improve your 30-second first impression?

3. What traits do you look for to determine if an individual is coachable or not?

4. What are three ways to create a more robust positive image when interacting with others?

5. Consider how you behave when no one is watching (or so you think).

6. What can you do to make your workplace "recruit ready?"

7. Is your nonverbal communication style vaulting you forward, or is it holding you back from opportunity?

10

White-Tailed Deer and Career Progression

We all remember what it was like to be hired for our first job out of college, to be excited to put our knowledge to the test and prove that we were not only ready for this challenge, but eager to advance quickly up that corporate ladder.

As you and I now know, new colleges grads don't realize that there is no substitute for work-related experience. You need time to engage in growth within your career. Just like a plant needs proper feeding, water, and a little bit of love to grow, you too need to experience this process at work. Through great mentoring, failures, rejections, success stories, and challenges, you will undoubtably receive more knowledge than you ever received in the classroom. This growth process allows you not just to survive, but to thrive.

As a leader, you play a vital role as you mentor the people on your team. This is a big step you need to understand in order to develop a strong and sustainable culture within your organization. A growth process needs to be collectively addressed daily, by both the supervisor and the employee. Only then will you and your organization be ready to sustain long-term success and a strong culture within your organization.

Ready to Change the World

While most will agree our college days were enjoyable, the responsibilities we had were minimal compared to the "real world" of employment that was just over the horizon. Attending class, preparing for exams, maybe even a bit of social indulging on occasional Friday evenings were the routine many of us followed.

As college years come to an end and graduation inches closer, reality starts to set in. You now have to become an "adult." Hopefully, the nervousness of entering the "real" world transitions into excitement for the next chapter in life. You're ready to apply the schooling and classroom theories to make your mark in the workplace, ready to change the world!

When I reflect back on my first few post-college years, I realize how much I thought I knew as my professional career began to take shape. I finished my college days of playing baseball and set out to start a career as a physical education teacher and coach. I thought about how easy it was going be.

I figured those established teachers and coaches had no idea I played baseball and how much I knew. I could out-teach and out-coach these guys in my sleep. I was going to teach my players bunt defenses, first and third offensive plays, how to hit and run—skills I figured those old-school guys never even thought about.

I was young—full of "piss and vinegar" as the saying goes—and was ready to outwork everyone around me.

Find a Way to Kindle Your Passion

Don't get me wrong, it's great to have all that energy and excitement to tackle a task. How many times have we heard this: "If you love the job you do, then it doesn't really feel like work!" I was fortunate to be in this position, as I was working in a field that I had great passion for.

What does passion mean for most of us? We try to find a major in college that interests us and that will lead to work in our chosen field. We all hope to have the interests we gained in college transition into meaningful experiences and a rewarding career that we are excited to pursue. Striving to make an impact on our field of employment becomes our goal. This is the main reason we search for a career that is satisfying and hope that our choice leads us to be passionate in what we do.

> You have the ability to ignite passion in others.

However, many times I hear that people are not satisfied with their jobs or the field they have chosen to pursue.

"I wish I studied harder." "I should've majored in . . . " "Man, I would've loved to do what you do."

Way too often people believe they are missing the boat. Yet there are many ways to find passion in your current field. For instance, very few people have a job that doesn't involve some personal interaction, and this provides a great opportunity to make an immense impact on others. Whether with co-workers, clients, or competitors, you can have an influence on people who can ignite and fuel your passion.

This is not easy, and it certainly takes a positive thinker with a great attitude—that optimistic attitude necessary to be infectious. You need to find a way to navigate the ups and downs, including those Monday morning blues.

Take Your Time—You Don't Know It All Just Yet

We certainly need passion to drive our interests and make a positive impact on those around us, but this can lead to a false sense of confidence. We think we know it all, sometimes better than the individuals we consider past their prime.

Ego starts to creep in: "I mean, come on, how does this old guy know about the technology I just learned in college?" (In Chapter 13 we'll take an in-depth look at the importance and the pitfalls that come with a big ego.) I call it being "young and dumb." When we've just started our first job, we have so much energy and passion, and we believe we're ready for any challenge. In reality, we have absolutely no idea how much we have to learn or how much we need to grow. We haven't failed or succeeded yet, or dealt with controversy or obstacles.

The presence of a large ego at a young age clouds our ability to learn valuable lessons by observing others. If only we could take a moment to lose that ego as we engage our co-workers and absorb as much knowledge as we can from the people around us. When the right mindset is present, experiences allow us to grow at a steady rate. This ultimately helps us develop into the leaders we are capable of becoming, who can handle crisis management, and help foster success within the organization.

The Beauty and Life of a White-Tailed Deer

I want to share a story that illustrates the way age, along with experience, can help you become a successful leader and thrive personally as well.

I grew up in rural northwest New Jersey, in a family that valued and respected the land. (Yes, New Jersey is more than casinos and the Jersey turnpike. There are mountains, lakes, and farmland too.) We farmed vegetables, raised chickens for their eggs, and hunted both small and large game for some of the meat we ate. I learned the skills of hunting rabbits, pheasants, turkeys and the whitetail deer native to that part of the country. Family members taught me to shoot accurately, be stealthy in the woods, and always look for the signs that wildlife was present. I understand that not everyone agrees with hunting, and unfortunately the actions of some people have given hunting a bad name. But I was brought up not only to respect the land, but to treat any game with the utmost respect.

The most beautiful animal I have had the chance to see in the wild, the whitetail deer, is considered one of the most difficult to harvest, even in places like Pennsylvania and New Jersey, where any cornfield on a fall evening is likely to boast massive herds of deer. The whitetail has keen senses of sight, hearing, and smell to alert the herd to any nearby dangers.

The name whitetail comes from the Native Americans, who relied on this animal for survival. When the deer are alarmed by a situation they deem dangerous, they will "throw" up their tails, which is about 10 inches long. The underside is bright white, like a fresh snowfall. This "flag," as it's known, alerts the other deer to hightail it out of there.

The bucks, or male deer, go through a few stages of growth over the course of their lives, and can be visually differentiated from the does, or female deer, by their antlers, which get larger as they grow older. Their antlers are usually measured in terms of points—the number of prongs. The more the points, the bigger and older the buck.

The Whitetail Life Cycle as Metaphor

When I study the whitetail's life cycle, I see a parallel to the working lifespan of a human, from the college graduate fresh out of school to the retiring employee:

- At 18–24 months, the male deer is "young and dumb," growing rapidly and making mistakes. They are small in stature, and their antlers usually measure 4–6 points.
  - In the workforce, this is the person right out of college, 23–30 years old, full of energy and ready to conquer any task. They jump into situations eagerly, sometimes prematurely, and don't always think things through. A lot of ego is also present: they believe they have it all figured out.
- At 2 to 5 years old, young bucks are beginning to mature, getting bigger, healthier, and smarter. Antlers usually measure 6 to 8 points and are starting to develop more mass. They were fortunate to survive the mistakes they made, which helped them learn. They also begin to listen better, looking for ways to process what they hear to help them survive.
  - In the workforce, the 30- to 45-year-old employee is now figuring things out—learning, growing, and finding that observing others, particularly veteran employees, can be a great resource for development.
- At 5 years old, the bucks are in their prime, carrying a massive set of antlers, measuring 10–14 points, wider than their chest. Past experiences, knowledge, and wisdom have made them smart and elusive, able to evade hunters, predators, and pitfalls.

- In the workforce, this represents the 45- to 65-year-old worker, someone whose work and life experiences have helped in the evolution to become the CEO, the boss, the top of the corporate chain. Many others look to these people for advice and guidance. They're also the ones who take responsibility for the ups and downs of the entire organization.

- From age 7 to the end of life, the buck starts to get smaller. They're not considered the alpha anymore. As they age, they become slower, and those antlers actually reduce in size, down to 6–8 points.

  - Unfortunately, as much as we hate to admit it, this also is a part of the human life cycle. There comes a time when people realize it might be time to bow out and retire. They mentored many people inside the organization and certainly left the business better than when they arrived. They know it is time to turn their knowledge over to the younger buck.

Growing from Rookie to Veteran

A good friend of mine from Maine, Keven Ireland, is one of the most successful and driven people I have ever met. Keven thrives in the company he works for, rising from a junior salesperson to a few steps away from president of a Fortune 500 company. Keven is also a world-class whitetail hunter.

Hunting whitetail is hard. Some people go years without even seeing a deer, especially in a state like Maine, where the winters are so harsh that many deer simply can't survive. Only the strong, intelligent, and resilient whitetail can make it past a few years in this environment. The deer there are so flighty and sparse that it is rare even to see one. When you hunt in Maine, every a little slipup causes a deer to flee. Stepping on a broken stick, coughing, dropping your flashlight while climbing a tree stand—all send any chance of glimpsing a deer out the window.

Hunting can be a great outlet, along with providing a passion for nature. It takes years of practice and failures to hone the skills necessary to be successful. The growth from rookie hunter to seasoned veteran can take a lifetime. But that process can be accelerated if you choose to work hard at it. My buddy Keven became an expert hunter much quicker than others because he has unbelievable drive. He possesses that gene that makes him study, work, practice, and prepare more than most people are willing to. This makes him a successful hunter, a successful and valuable employee, and a successful person.

Like a whitetail or an employee, over time a hunter will also go through transitions. In the first few years, the hunter feels that harvesting any wild game, especially a whitetail, is a monumental feat, due to missed shots, dropped flashlights, and cellphones you forgot to silence while sitting hours in a tree stand, only to see a whitetail running from you. As you become a more seasoned hunter, you learn from those mistakes, leading to more success. And after many years, some hunters tend to be less interested in harvesting more game and instead want to challenge themselves, to harvest a much more mature and experienced deer.

Remember the growth process of the whitetail? The animal is also learning from its mistakes. A young buck might slip up during the rut, the mating season of the animal. Focused on a young doe, the buck is not paying attention to danger signs like sounds from people or cars, which can lead to a lethal outcome.

The whitetails with the instinct, know-how, and a bit of luck grow from these mistakes, and evolve into beautiful specimens. They are known as Boone and Crockett whitetails, the term given to a massive, record deer, far bigger in stature than most of its peers. The only chance you ever have to harvest a five-year-old whitetail is to possess the knowledge, know-how, and smarts. The ability to work hard and deal with multiple failures and setbacks needs to be constant a mindset.

Although I grew up hunting, I did not become a true hunter until I met Keven. He showed me things I would never think of to increase my chances of becoming a veteran: keeping detailed logs, tracking patterns of the moon, planting food plots, locating bedding and transition areas. Hunting season runs from late October through the middle of November. Keven amazed me with the countless hours he put into hunting, even prior to the season. He starts his process of "scouting" in April, once the Maine forest begins to slowly lose its constant blanket of snow. His success rate with Boone and Crockett deer is remarkable, especially for Maine.

If you remember my earlier story about my shoelaces in Chapter 5, you'll recall that I don't believe in either bad or good luck. However, most likely the mature buck acquired great wisdom and stature through a little good fortune. He might have ignored the sounds of danger, putting him in the crosshairs of young hunter, only to have that hunter shoot and miss. Possibly the car he ran in front of happened to swerve and avoided contact. Through these experiences, that deer became seasoned, avoiding future mishaps.

Persistence

Most hunters quit the sport for two reasons. First, they get frustrated, because it's not as easy to hunt a whitetail as they thought. Second, they get bored. It takes years of experience through a lot of tedium to have any chance of success and they don't want to make that commitment.

The hunter who does make that commitment is rare, and that's Keven. He prepares, researches, and is willing to put in the extra effort to be successful. He works efficiently and effectively. He's calm in his approach, never letting his emotions get too high or too low. He's *persistent* in his pursuit of success. His traits and values make him stand out among others.

When this kind of persistence transitions into the work-place, you have employees who shine, who grow and move quickly up the corporate ladder. They are the ones willing to go the extra mile to strive for success.

You see the fruits of Keven's labor in each hunting season.

You Pick, and Mentor, Your Team

So, how does this relate to leadership? Part of being a great leader is to understand that your success and failures are directly impacted by who you surround yourself with:

Who are you hiring?

Who are you allowing to be on your team?

Who deserves the promotion and who needs a bit more time to age?

> You get to choose the team.

You are the coach, the CEO, the supervisor, the boss, so you get to choose the players. You get to choose the team. You certainly get to hire your employees. Given the choice, of course you'd hire all the "five-year-old bucks" you could. They can be quite difficult to find, but sometimes you might have a few future ones already with you. They could be members of your current team or organization and require a little mentoring and a bit of time to mature. They just have not yet had the chance to grow into what they might become.

Recognize the Future of Five-Year-Old Whitetails When Hiring

Our role as leader requires us to surround ourselves with the right people when building our organization. We first need to find people we think have the traits to be successful. Then we must help them grow, similar to that beautiful whitetail deer.

They will need nurturing, advice, room to grow and room to fail. They need mentoring and you will undoubtedly find frustration in this process as a leader. Your role is to guide your employees every day, coupled with empowering them, to develop at your side.

However, your own approach in the hiring process is vital as you navigate the challenges of putting a team together. Your lack of preparation during this process, failing to bring the right people to your team with the ability to develop values, can cause major strains on your organization.

Realize some of your employees and team members will never grow to become the five-year-old buck. If you, their leader, work hard to hire, mentor, empower, and grow your employees, you can establish a consistent success rate. Eventually, your skills and devotion to leadership will allow you to develop a few of those five-year-old whitetails that can be your best employees, earners, players or captains.

Roles Change

A tough job that a leader has to be willing, and capable, to perform is recognizing when it is time to change the role of one of your employees. When you determine the five-year-old whitetail has grown into that seven-year-old, it is time revisit your organizational puzzle. Remember, everyone can be a piece of your puzzle, and those puzzle pieces will change.

Keep a keen eye out for the times you need to redefine the individual roles of your team. This can prove to be difficult; some people on your team have unbelievable experience and knowledge. They might require additional training or a role change within the organization. It is vital to organizational long-term success that you develop the skill set to empower your team, no matter what level of competency each employee holds—especially when dealing with your veteran staff members.

> Your job, as their leader, is to nurture and
> mentor them each day.

A seasoned employee can bring tremendous value. Much like the development you fostered with the very young buck, you must find a way to continue to view the value in the older, seasoned veteran. Keep in mind it will be tough to get some to change habits. This is another responsibility you have as a leader—to mentor all of the people of your organization, including the veteran employees. Yes, old dogs can learn new tricks, but only if you are willing to as well, along with investing the time and energy to lead your entire team.

Veteran employees have great knowledge and know-how, but might lack in some other area. Maybe it's technology, or passion for the grind of the competitive work environment. However, they should be celebrated for the loyalty, dedication, experience, and service they bring to the organization. They can bring great value, holding roles of mentoring teammates, that can benefit others thoughout the entire organization.

Recognize the value each person brings to your team, no matter whether they are just starting within the company, or nearing retirement.

Be the Growth Process for Them

For organizational success, leaders must recognize their role as mentors to everyone on the team. Understand that not everyone around you possesses the same abilities or knowledge, and everyone is at a different developmental stage in their respective careers. Your job as their leader is to nurture and mentor them each day.

And you get the opportunity to see them grow into that beautiful whitetail deer.

Coach's Challenge

1. What is your passion? How can it relate to your job?

2. Can you find out the passions of your team members? What can you do to fuel their passion?

3. Can you focus on one thing at your workplace to be persistent with?

4. When hiring new employees, what steps can you develop to recognize values you consider important to develop future young bucks?

5. What are you or your organization doing to attract strong whitetails?

6. Develop a plan to spend time mentoring your veteran employees and explain the value they have within your organization.

11

Fall Forward When You Fail—and You're Gonna Fail!

So far, I have pointed out all the values, traits, and practices it takes to be a better leader for your team. When you invest in your team, you have the ability to foster long-term success. But there will be many days things don't go your way. All the preparation you put into a project can be quickly washed away due to factors you can't control. Setbacks and failures will certainly happen and are a natural part of growth and development. So get ready for it, as you undoubtably will fail. Yet with the proper mindset, it becomes an engine to drive you to becoming a quality leader or successful person.

Try a little test to see just how many people with great success stories have failed over and over again. Google "Successful people who failed." It's an impressive list; you rarely find a highly successful person who hasn't failed, sometimes in remarkable ways.

When failure happens, you can't blame those "shoulda, woulda, coulda" explanations. It is very important to develop the ability of keeping your emotions from getting the best of you when facing failure. Rather, you need the ability to refocus and limit any damage caused by failure. Explore new methods to build off of setbacks and learn to appreciate failure as great teaching tools for personal growth.

In and Out of Your Control

Failure happens in two different forms. It can involve failure to manage variables around you that are beyond your control. For example, when a competitor in your field of business significantly undercuts prices to win business from a company you are both vying for, or an umpire makes a poor call that goes against your team, you can't do anything to affect the outcome of these situations. Setbacks that lead to a failed situation will undoubtably happen, and can be quite frustrating, especially when they are out of your control.

I learned this the hard way early in my collegiate coaching career. On one particular day, when I was a first-year coach, my team was in a heated battle with our conference rival. As with most baseball games, there was a close play at first base and I believed our runner beat the throw from the defense and should have been called safe. I did the typical posturing and headed out of the dugout to the field to confront the umpire about my displeasure in his call. Coaches do this plenty of times in the game; it's something of a ritual, a form of defending your players by sticking up for what you believe is right.

Being young, and a bit dumb (like the young whitetail buck from Chapter 10), I sprinted out to get in the umpire's face. I was going to show my players just how to argue the call and prove to them I had their backs. Boy, was I heated—face to face, spit flying, and some very choice words.

Then, I got dumped, meaning I was asked to leave the field and stop coaching. Yet I continued to put on a show, kicking dirt, covering up home plate, forcing the umpire to bend down and brush it off when all the dust settled that I was literally causing.

I certainly couldn't have controlled the outcome of that play, but in making my point, I got tossed. Now the team didn't have my leadership and guidance for the rest of the game. Worse off, my emotions got the best of me.

The following Monday, I was summoned to the office of Bob Byrnes, my athletic director. There he sat, back to me and feet up on the cabinet behind his desk, hands folded behind his head.

"Did you get ejected this weekend?" he asked

"Yea, Bob, but it wasn't my fault! That umpire screwed us."

"Here is the report that was written. Did you call him these things?" Bob spun in his chair, with fire in his eyes.

"Well, I was kinda heated and I don't really remember everything I said." Now my shoulders sank.

"This is not what I want out of our head coach! Don't embarrass me and the school!" he shouted from deep within his stomach.

Bob went on to suspend me for a game to make his point, a well-deserved punishment.

The failure caused by that one call the umpire didn't get right led to a greater setback: me being absent, as the team's leader, for more games. My emotions got the best of me in a situation I really had no control over.

To this day, when an umpire makes a bad call, I still trot out to defend my players and follow baseball etiquette. By calmly making my point and discussing how I feel, the umpire's call still doesn't change. However, I have learned this approach now gives our team a better chance to get the next call to go our way.

So, even though I don't have control of what an umpire thinks, I can build a tiny bit of a relationship the right way, in hopes to get the next subjective call go my team's way.

Another form of failure happens when your unpreparedness or lack of attention to details affects the outcome of things over which you do have an influence. This might be how well you prepare for a test in a class you're enrolled in, or a sales pitch presentation your boss asked you to prepare. You control these variables, and if you choose to invest in the core values you or your organization has in place, not only will your rate of failure decrease, but you are better prepared to pivot in a positive direction when setbacks occur. Don't blame a wild night out with friends as a reason your work didn't get done. This was a choice you made that impacted the result.

When considering the inevitable failures you will surely face, recognize which situations you can control and which you can't. Tackle the ones you can, so you increase your ability to be successful. And remember to look for the teaching moment in every setback.

People Want You to Fail

As you grow in your professional role and climb the corporate ladder, you may sense that some people grow jealous and even become resentful of your success. A colleague who was a one-time friend now views your advancement as a threat, and can even become an enemy.

> Look within yourself to develop a mindset that will allow you to grow and flourish.

There will always be foes and even friends who want to see you fail. This desire is beyond your control; don't waste time proving your worth to them because it will turn out to be fruitless. Such people can wreak havoc on those around you, particularly those you entrust to make up a productive and healthy culture.

You probably expect your competitors to want you to fail, but when it comes from people within your own organization, it can result in cracks in the company's culture and core values. Don't invest much time or energy in the doomsayers who try to infiltrate your team. Look within yourself to develop a mind-set that will allow you to grow and flourish. It can be a great self-motivator to use their negativity to inspire your own optimistic attitude.

Fail and Move Forward

Failure in the workplace and in everyday life is inevitable. No matter how big or small, setbacks are going to happen to everyone, so you might as well prepare for them.

We have discussed the importance of how a positive attitude can influence those around you. The same holds true when faced with adversity. Without a positive outlook and a belief that setbacks hold value, you can easily fall into the trap of becoming a negative Nellie. When you allow your emotions to dictate decisions and you neglect the valuable lessons from such failures, you ultimately miss the opportunity to use the important information gained by failures to help guide you to future success.

As previously mentioned, the optimist demonstrates how, during fragile times, a positive outlook can result in more productive outcomes. Conversely, a pessimistic attitude will more likely result in negative outcomes. It can be difficult to remain optimistic in times of failure, yet you must find it deep within yourself to accomplish this thought process and always choose to look for a positive outcome from a negative situation.

Get busy living, or get busy dying.

Here is a great example of an optimistic outlook that produced a positive end result. Many days as the baseball coach at the University of Maine, I would get the field ready to play a home game in early March by having the entire team pitch in to shovel it clear of snow. Inevitably, just as the team finished the task, another snowstorm would hit, with a predicted 16 inches still to come. What a great opportunity to bond as a team and shovel the field again!

"Hey, fellas, no one would even attempt to do what we're doing, so that makes us tougher than everyone!" I would shout.

Believe me, it sucks to have to keep shoveling that damn field over and over when all you want to do is practice and play, but I would embellish just how great it was. I tried to be the ultimate optimist.

Having the same approach when failure happens enables you to refocus more quickly and get busy accomplishing. If you ask many of the people I've been around, both former players and groups I've presented to, they will tell you about a movie line I use all the time. On my list of top three movies of all time sits *The Shawshank Redemption*, based on a Stephen King novella. (By the way, Stephen is a UMaine grad.) In the movie, the character played by Morgan Freeman is describing what you need to do when you're stuck in prison. He says in life you have to "Get busy living, or get busy dying."

Well, that's how I feel about failure. Take it head on and tell yourself it can be a great motivator and path to success.

Convince yourself it's going to make you better, stronger, and tougher. No matter how crazy it might sound, you have to believe in your ability to adjust, learn, and grow from failure. It is essential to you and your team's toughness and success.

Be Responsible and Positive in Times of Failure

Be forewarned, ego can sometimes get in the way of springboarding off failures. Resist the temptation to blame others or things that are out of your control. In Chapter 13, we'll explore ideas about ego and the role it can play when building confidence, and we'll also address the crucial step of suppressing that same ego within your organization or team. The same goes for failed outcomes for yourself.

A true leader takes responsibility for setbacks, recognizes that they will occur, and prepares for them. Furthermore, a good leader will have an answer for failures that occur when it isn't their fault. If someone on their team makes a mistake, they come to their defense, taking responsibility for not aiding in their preparation. Your true toughness and energy are tested and the opportunity arises to demonstrate these important values to your team.

I have a great baseball example of exactly this. The team captain of the highly successful 2018 Stetson Hatters was Brooks Wilson. Brooksie was a two-way player; meaning he hit in our offensive lineup and also pitched. In fact, he was the closer on that club, which meant he came in the last inning or two and slammed the door, trying very hard not to give up any runs, let alone base runners.

In one particular game, the score was 3–2 going into the bottom of the ninth inning, with the Hatters on top. Brooksie came into the game as the pitcher to do what he does best—close it out and get the save. He had the first batter he faced sitting at an 0–2 count, pumping two strikes right by the lead-off hitter that inning. The third pitch he threw was designed to go inside to the hitter, hoping for a swing and a miss for strike three. Brooksie executed the pitch, hitting the location he wanted and induced a weak ground ball to the shortstop. As the shortstop charged in to field the ball and make a throw to first base for the out, he let the ball go under his glove for an error.

Now Brooksie could have thrown his hands up in disgust, showing frustration and poor body language, because he had done what he was supposed to do to get the first out. Instead, Brooks turned around and told the player, "Hey, don't worry about that, it wasn't your fault. I shoulda made a better pitch and the ball shoulda never been hit to you! Now, let's get the next hitter and I'm gonna strike him out, or you get to now start a double play with the next ground ball."

The short stop's body language instantly changed. His head had been hanging low and arms were on his hips, but now both perked up. As he heard Brooks's words, he pounded his glove and returned to his position for the next play.

When he faced the next batter, Brooks induced yet another ground ball, this time to the second basemen. He was able to field it properly, flipping it to the shortstop for out number one at second base and complete the double play for the second out. Brooks gave a nod to the shortstop and went on to strike out the next batter for out number three and closed out the game for a win.

He was a true leader, and a huge part of that season's success. His ability to take responsibility when it wasn't his fault resonated throughout our organization. The setback dealt to him in that game gave him the opportunity to take responsibility for something that he either didn't have control over or had nothing to do with. His actions brought the group together, built trust in him, and energized the rest of the team to get the job done the next time the opportunity arose.

> Showing positivity in challenging times and filling your mind with optimistic ideas can encourage others to adopt that same process.

Taking responsibility during times of failure and crisis management yields a valuable opportunity to showcase the true toughness and energy we addressed earlier. The ability to own failure when it's not your fault demonstrates to your organization just how committed you are, and surely it will begin to rub off on others. Showing positivity in challenging times and filling your mind with optimistic ideas can encourage others to adopt that same process. Your organization will be able to prevail through the ups and downs we all deal with on a daily basis.

Remember that powerful saying, "Tough times don't last, but tough people do." When dealt failure, mentally tough individuals are positive, resilient, and take responsibility for the group. They show humility when success happens for them, but take responsibility when failure strikes. The noise created by detractors doesn't derail them; it energizes them. To become a great leader, it is vital to understand the value of failure and how it can be a necessary path in the growth process.

Coach's Challenge

1. Can you take a clear negative situation at your workplace and "spin" it into an opportunity to be positive?

2. Can you name a time you were able to be mentally tough in a time of failure, taking responsibility for a setback?

3. Name a failure that happened in your work or personal life that was out of your control.

4. Name a failure you had control over where you could have altered the outcome.

5. In the future, find a way to take responsibility of one setback at your workplace that was the responsibility of someone on your team.

12

Keep Chopping Wood: Pressure versus Preparation

Most of us strive to find an occupation that we enjoy and have a passion for. Additionally, we hope our workplace and co-workers are just as satisfying. When this combination transpires, you are grateful to have a job and people within that organization you enjoy.

For us to continue to operate at our place of employment at a high level, we engage in many of the values and traits explored throughout the book. An essential trait to add to your repertoire is the ability to prepare for your next steps. This is a widespread concept; the Boy Scouts have used this motto since their inception: be prepared.

But do you really look at this idea and invest the proper amount of time to actually prepare for your day? Most people don't go all in. They tend to half-prepare, thinking they already know the information, and because they are experienced at their job, they figure they don't need to waste time. They aren't willing to go the extra mile and find ways to educate, or reeducate, themselves.

These are the folks who feel pressure, created because they failed to properly prepare. Whether it's a recertification exam required for work, a business sales pitch to a potential client, or a practice for a big game, failure to prepare at 100 percent effort will result in feeling some pressure when the "game" is on. Ironically, the stress and tension that accompanies an unequipped approach to a task is something that each person has control over because they can spend time preparing, allowing them to manage the level of pressure. So there is no excuse to underprepare.

Relationships Lead to Wins

When I first got into coaching at the Division I level, I was convinced the way to win was all about recruiting and teaching. I worked hard to get the most talented players to come to my school, and I worked them very hard to improve. Of course, this will always be true; you do need some strong horses to pull the wagon. However, as times change, so does the role of many coaches in terms of managing those players. This is equally important within the business sector.

Eventually, I learned that an increasingly important role in the coaching world is that athletic directors require coaches to aid in development work, philanthropy, and fundraising. This might be for large capital projects, such as a new stadium, or simply budget relief to help offset costs to run the program. You can't meet an alum or donor for the first time and ask them to invest in you and the program with a financial gift. It takes time, and lots of it, to cultivate these individuals. You have to really get to know them, and likewise they to know you.

A solid relationship has to form. Eventually, if this connection is present, most people will want to be involved in your vision and invest in *you*. In fact, if you fully invest in building relationships, rather than having to ask donors for money, inevitably they will ask you how they can help. In one form or another, if you want to have success at the Division I level, coaches will engage in some form of philanthropic work. This is the "other" side of coaching that many do not realize is vital to the success of the program.

So, the experiences I have been fortunate enough to be in and the people I engaged with have led me to meet some of the most interesting and successful people in the world. In fact, it is a major factor in why I wanted to write a book. Having the opportunity to meet to an alum who was a CEO of a major corporation or a small business owner who built an empire from ground up, I quickly realized their stories are exactly what I was trying to teach young men and grow them into good, tough, competitive ball players. Their path to success revolved around great values in terms of leadership.

The Alfond Way

One of the first people I met when I took the UMaine baseball job was Harold Alfond. His success story is quite remarkable: he built a major shoe company from the ground up.

In 1956, he purchased an old mill in Dexter, Maine, and founded Dexter Shoe Company, producing shoes to supply stores such as Sears, JC Penney, Spiegel, and Montgomery Ward & Co. Dexter was successful from the beginning, and Harold decided to go into the "branded" business. He developed a line of shoes under the Dexter name, hired a sales force, and began selling to independent shoe stores across the country.

With the growth and expansion of Dexter Shoes, Alfond would be forever credited with the invention of the factory outlet store. Factories sometimes made mistakes in the hand production process of shoe making. The factory-damaged shoes would be sold at steep discounts to workers, who would then turn around and resell them for five times their cost.

Alfond saw the potential in reselling factory seconds and opened up his factory to the general public for sales. Eventually, Alfond folded into the sales inventory shoes that simply weren't selling quick enough. With growing popularity, Alfond began putting up his factory outlet stores throughout New England. Other manufacturers followed suit, building their own outlet stores neighboring Dexter. Innovative thinking, an understanding of business, and a willingness to take calculated risks enabled Alfond in early 1990 to sell Dexter to Berkshire Hathaway for over $400 million in stock.

He clearly knew how to run a corporation. And Harold loved sports. He attended every UMaine hockey and football game he could. He recognized the value of competition that comes from a sporting contest, coupled with the extremely hard work it takes to be a constant winner, and infused those principles into his company. After he sold the Dexter Shoe Company to Warren Buffet for that crazy amount of Berkshire Hathaway stock, he went on to invest in many other companies and projects that built his empire.

That day when he walked into my office to introduce himself and shake my hand, I asked him to tell me his story. How had he become so successful starting with a shoe store in a small sleepy town in Maine? He asked me to take a seat, open up my ears, and get ready for a great ride. He was about to give me a great lesson in leadership, a lesson always to keep chopping wood, even when you think you have enough.

"Keep Chopping Wood"

Harold emphasized the importance not only of putting in a day of hard work, but the ability to outwork others.

"You people from away need to understand these winters up here in Maine are cold and long," he explained. I later found out native Mainers refer to people from out of state as "from away."

Just when you think you have it all figured out, that's when you most likely will fall short. He explained the importance of practicing, preparing, and overpreparing for every situation you put yourself in. Whether that means coaching a team, running a business, spending quality time with family, and, of course, gathering wood to heat your house, a positive and successful day was more obtainable with good old elbow grease.

"You may think you have enough wood stacked in the garage, but you'll likely fall short. So don't ever stop chopping. Don't ever stop working. Don't ever stop learning," Harold advised.

Harold's story of the importance to keep chopping wood literally happened to me the previous winter. And boy was he right!

If you've ever lived in the north—especially a place like Maine—you know how long and harsh the winters can be, with relentlessly cold days where the sun rises at 7 a.m. and it's completely dark at 4 p.m. For months many people go to work and return home in darkness. It can be a bit depressing.

But another reality is you get those warm, cozy, snowy weekends sitting by the wood stove. There is nothing like the heat that comes off a good wood-burning stove. It relaxes you, and it can be a huge money saver from the rising prices of heating costs.

So, like many, we burned wood to heat our house. The other thing about burning wood is the satisfaction of gathering your yearly supply.

I always found it funny that the big topic in summer and early fall is "Did ya get your wood laid in the dooryard?" (A dooryard is what a Mainer calls the area of the yard near the most-used door of the home.) Now, some take the easy way out and pay premium dollar for something that is right in their backyard, up to $200 for a cord of wood. (A cord is a tightly stacked pile of wood, 4 feet high by 4 feet wide and 8 feet long.) On average, if using wood as the primary heat source, the typical house can burn up to 4–6 cords of wood each winter.

I decided I would rather invest in a quality chainsaw, and borrow a homemade log splitter from a buddy of mine and save some money by doing the work myself. It's also a great outlet for the satisfaction of physical labor.

Off I went to find good hardwood trees to cut, split, stack, and season (dry). Little did I know the number of trees, and the amount of work, it took to get one cord of wood! I thoroughly enjoyed the process, but it was time consuming and laborious.

My first winter, I made the rookie move of getting what I thought was enough wood laid in the garage. Man, did it look impressive! After days and days of hard work, I had about 3 cords. That year, as winter approached, I was excited to fire up that stove in late October, as the leaves were all down off the trees. I was even more excited when the heating oil bill came the next month, and it was practically nothing! My hard work surely helped my bank account. But as the months went on, my wood pile began to shrink.

"When the heck does this Maine winter end?" I thought around February. And in March, it happened. I burned my last bit of wood. Naturally, I couldn't truck though three feet of snow to harvest more; it would not be dry and seasoned. And if you try to burn "wet" or newly chopped wood, all it does is smoke and does not burn very hot.

So I called around to a couple of wood businesses and asked if I could get a cord delivered. Boy were they happy for my call.

"Hello, sir. I saw you sell wood and actually I called you last summer to see if I could get a few cords from you," I said sheepishly.

"Yep, I'd be happy to bring ya some. I have a few cords left. I can get it out to ya by Tuesday. $800 a cord."

What! That $200 quote for seasoned, delivered cord I received the previous summer was long gone.

"Supply and demand, my friend" he told me.

Rookie mistake. So, all the money I saved in heating oil I just gave back for two extra cords.

Mr. Alfond taught me a valuable lesson that day in my office. He shared the story of his success to make sure I would not only take advice, but would listen to the experiences of others. I only wish he told me his "Keep chopping wood" story when I first moved to Maine, and not after my first winter. I would have saved a bundle of money!

I knew how important Harold Alfond was to UMaine athletics and all he had given in gifts. I also knew he did not support just UMaine, but many other programs as well. Heck, there must be a dozen Alfond arenas or stadiums around New England and even in Florida! When I had that valuable one-hour meeting with Harold, I asked him a simple yet important question. "How did you make Dexter Shoes so successful?"

Keep chopping wood, he told me. Just when you think you've done enough, something will happen that you could have been prepared for. A long winter. A friend in need. An employee requiring guidance. Many things will come upon you as you navigate through daily trials and tribulations within the workplace. What he was telling me was to keep working.

> Just when you think you've done enough, something will happen that you could have been prepared for.

You may think you have it figured out, or have gotten in front of the job, then your competitor outworks you. Outcompetes you. Learn to compete with yourself. Challenge yourself every day. Just as important, Harold taught me the lesson of self-reward. How fulfilling is it when you finish a hard day's work, to step back and evaluate the rewards. That huge pile of wood in the shed from six hours of chopping really makes you want to crack open a cold one, sit back, and stare at your masterpiece. And this becomes addictive. You want to top what you did the previous day. You strive for more success. Become enthralled with the competition within yourself, and certainly your competitors. Use any setbacks as motivation to go forward. Like we said earlier, fall forward with failures; setbacks and obstacles act as great lessons.

So, as Harold illustrated that day though his story of success, it's essential to keep working hard. Never lose the persistence it takes to get better, especially when you think you're on top of the world. There are many quotes and stories about hard work. But simply put: keep chopping wood. Your employees see it. Your players see it. That work ethic is contagious. They will follow your lead as their leader.

"Sharpen Your Axe"

After that wonderful day with Harold, I next met probably the most important person in relation to Maine baseball,

Larry Mahaney. Harold and Larry were very close; they saw their respective businesses grow in the same era. Their families intertwined, and they quite frequently vacationed together. The baseball complex at UMaine was named for him: Mahaney Diamond, Mahaney Dome, Mahaney Clubhouse. In fact, like Harold Alfond, multiple sports fields in Maine are named for the Mahaney family.

Larry was a tremendous athlete in his days as a high school football, basketball, and baseball player. He was raised about as far north in Maine as you can go, in Aroostook County—potato-growing country. Larry grew up on a potato farm, working for his family. He went on to become a very successful coach at Brewer High School in the 1950s, winning many championships. His tough, blue-collar style motivated many young athletes to be their best. He eventually left coaching and entered the business sector, working for a very successful heating oil company, Webber Energy Fuels. Eventually, through his tenacious work ethic, management style, and leadership, he rose to become the president and CEO of Webber.

Soon after my visit with Mr. Alfond, a stocky, fit man in his 70s walked though my office door. Larry was quite different than the soft-spoken Harold Alfond. He seemed almost like an oil tycoon from Texas! He introduced himself, sat across from me, and threw his feet up on the front of the desk.

"I heard my good buddy Harold stopped by to visit with you. Well, he and I are heavily invested in UMaine athletics, and we want to help you be successful," he explained.

Some young coaches might let their ego take over and resist being told how to do their jobs. But I recognized the amount of success both Harold and Larry had, and realized I should shut up and listen. Larry warned me that he was a longtime baseball coach at Brewer and, unlike Harold, he knew about baseball. "Get ready for me to critique your coaching!" Great, I thought. I certainly had to be respectful; after all, his name was plastered all over the building and field.

He laughed. "Listen, I only want to help you, so don't get your panties in a bunch. Okay, now let's chop some wood." Chop wood? What the heck was he talking about? This had to be Harold's story he was about to tell me.

We went out to his old beat-up truck, and in the back was an 18-inch-diameter piece of wood, about 15 inches tall. He asked me to take it out of the truck and set it on top of another smaller piece next to it. So I put both pieces on the ground with the large one on top. After handling the wood, I noticed my hands all sticky with pine tar. Maine pine is very wet and sappy. In fact, no one burns it because it is too wet and burns too fast and does not put out the heat that a good hardwood like oak, cherry, or maple does.

The other thing to know about wet pine is that splitting it with an ax is very tough. Larry handed me an old, rusty, dull axe that looked like the person who swung it had missed many times—the handle by the axe head was dented and broken almost in half. "I bet I can split that piece of pine before you can." He boasted. Now, I was just past my 35th birthday, and probably in the best shape of my life. Larry, on the other hand was in his mid-70s. Naturally, I took the bet.

I took the axe, centered my body to make a huge overhead blow to the log, and made sure I squarely hit the middle of the piece of pine. *Wham!* I hit it perfectly. As I looked down, that axe stuck right into that piece, buried right up to the wooden handle under the blade. No split. Just a piece of wood with an axe sticking out of it. "Take another whack at it," he instructed me.

So I began the lengthy, tiresome process of freeing the axe from the wood. I pulled. I tugged. I even banged the piece of wood on the ground. I tried to kick that axe out of the log.

A good five minutes later, I was able to free that darn axe. Now I was sweating and breathing heavy. Blow number two. I figured the trick was to turn the log and hit in in an X pattern to split it in two. *Whack!* Same result. Five more minutes to free the axe, and now I was really starting to tire.

Larry then said he wanted a try. I didn't want this to end badly, with him getting hurt or even worse, having a heart attack. How would he accomplish something that I could not, and I was 40 years younger!

Larry went to the front of his truck and pulled out a case, which he set on the tailgate of his truck and opened. As I peered into that case, the sun hit a shiny object so bright that it blinded me for a bit. Larry pulled out a beautiful shiny hatchet. It looked like something from a museum or a very expensive item at L.L. Bean.

"I spent the past week not only hand sharping this axe, but polishing it as well," he told me. He then demonstrated how sharp it was by rubbing the blade up his arm, shaving off some of the white hair between his wrist and elbow. "Hours and hours. I used different sharpening stones, oils, and techniques my father taught me to sharpen tools."

He positioned the piece of pine with my huge X mark. After getting a good grip on his hatchet and taking a practice swing, he pulled it back ever so gently and made a downward swinging motion on the top of that wet, sappy log. *Whoosh!* He hit it square, with much less force than I did, and on the ground lay two half pieces of that log. I couldn't believe it. Did I "loosen" it up for him? How was it that my force could not get it done, but his short, swift tap easily split that piece of pine?

"Always sharpen your axe," told me. "Sharpening an axe can take a long time to get it right, but it will do wonders, saving you much more time, effort, and energy."

What Larry taught me that day was to make sure you are prepared, and practice, practice, practice.

> Make sure you are prepared, and practice, practice, practice.

Not all of life's obstacles are predictable, but we can be as prepared as possible though practice, hard work, effort, and thinking things through. Larry demonstrated that being prepared reduced the time, workload, and energy to get the job done. When it was go time in our bet, he was prepared and I wasn't. I did feel a bit of pressure to split that log, and he was a cool as a cucumber. In other words: keep your axe sharp at all times.

> Those who feel pressure are those who are not prepared.

This was the message I learned that day with Larry Mahaney: those who feel pressure are those who are not prepared. We've all been in pressure situations. Yet, when we've been successful in these instances, we had the ability to be calm, make sound decisions, and focus on performance.

With the Right Mindset, You Are Capable of Anything

We all know the saying that if you put your mind to it, you can do anything. Another example of this was a personal challenge I made with myself. Sometime around 2012, I became very involved in leadership within my organization, and was speaking to many businesses around the country on the topic.

A great friend of mine, Chris Farley (not the comedian) was a highly successful financial advisor in Maine. He was one of the most caring and giving people I have ever met, always there for you if you needed him and constantly had a positive outlook.

So, one night while sharing a beer, I told him of a presentation I had just made that week to a group of credit union people about leadership. I boasted about how with enough preparation, you can do anything. He wholeheartedly agreed and this prompted him to challenge me to a bet. He agreed to pay for me to take an online class to study for the health and life insurance exam, something every college grad must do when entering the financial world. If people passed and still wanted to work on that field, they would go on to take federally regulated tests to become full-fledged financial advisors.

I told him he was crazy—I didn't have the knowledge. Here I was with a physical education degree and a masters in educational leadership, not knowing the first thing about insurance. But Chris was such positive guy, he convinced me to take his bet.

So I studied in my "down" time—bus trips, plan rides, and the like. It took me almost six months to watch these lessons and do the practice tests, but I actually started to understand: whole life versus universal, fixed annuities, Medicare, and so on. I kept taking the practice exams and scoring higher and higher. Then, once October hit, I pulled the trigger and signed up for the actual test!

The day of the exam, I walked into the test center, and I must have been 20 years older than everyone else. Clearly, they were all recent college grads looking for their first job after this exam. Ninety questions in two hours, that was the task. Everyone looked nervous, but I felt really good about this. Once the test started, I was cruising through it. For many of the questions, I knew the answer before I even finished reading.

My 90th question came at just over the hour mark. I hit the send button on the computer, and my score popped up: 88 out of 90. As I stood up to leave, I saw others with that look on their face—like I cheated! Nope, just took a bet with a friend of mine about preparing.

Days later, in the mail, I received my certificate from the State of Maine. I was now licensed to work as a broker. Crazy to think that could happen, but the preparation was what got me to that step.

How did a baseball coach pass a life insurance exam? As crazy as this sounds, it's all about putting your mind to the task at hand, no matter how difficult it may seem. Finding a way to convince yourself you can accomplish a task, with a positive mindset and no negative thoughts allowed to creep in, can be a powerful tool for your success as a leader.

Taking Chris Farley's challenge motivated me to prepare for this once seemingly difficult task. If a baseball coach, with no experience in the insurance field, can pass a certification exam, think of how much you can accomplish in your own field of expertise. You need the proper frame of mind to approach the challenge.

Tackle Crisis Management Head On

We have to make sure the people we are influencing and mentoring every day understand that we have a difficult time being successful at "go time" if we don't prepare. I tell our players every day that we have to practice like we want to play in the game. If we practice with 50 percent effort, then that's how the game will go. Even if you think you're smarter and more talented than your competition, it's not possible to be consistently successful.

What we are striving for as leaders is to surround ourselves with talented individuals who value preparation—and not just with the obvious tasks, but the little things that make a group great. Do you take the extra time to practice the tasks at hand? Are you aware of your surroundings and (as we discussed earlier) your image? When this value becomes part of the culture within our organization, we start to be prepared. Sit back and analyze why this is important.

> Simply put, as leaders, we are preparing ourselves and our people for crisis management.

If we prepare for this, we can handle it when it happens. And it most certainly will happen. As a coach, you'll find that one of your players inevitably gets into trouble and you have to be consistent in your discipline.

Say you own a chain of coffee shops. All in the same day the ice machine breaks at one location, a shift worker doesn't show up at another store, and you get word from the main office that a manager is skimming off some profits and now not only do you have to fire that person, but you can't rely on them when you are short-staffed!

How about the ever-constant string of lawsuits business owners face? Every one of the many managers and business owners I have met, live with this threat hanging over their heads. They know it's coming, so best be prepared.

Crisis management.

The ones who are best prepared for it will be more successful when it happens. Think about the training that soldiers, firemen, police, EMT, rescue, and others do. Their preparation in a crisis can mean life or death. In the workforce, we surely do not have that type of pressure, but we still have the responsibility to deal with day-to-day work emergencies in the best possible way.

How you behave as a leader through your words, deeds, and actions will ultimately give you what becomes the "culture" of your organization. This is a monumental task, and many more fail at it than succeed. But those who can grind though the failures, and be best prepared for the trials and tribulations, will ultimately see success within their organization.

Those who feel the most pressure are those who fail to prepare.

Coach's Challenge

1. What ways can you cultivate the relationships with the people around you?
2. How can you be better at "chopping wood" at your workplace?
3. What tactics can you add to your daily routine to practice more, or "sharpen your axe?"
4. Can you find ways to reduce pressure? How will you prepare in your day?

13

Ego: You Better Have One

I am sure many of you have been told to practice being humble. It started early in our lives, when our parents wanted us to appreciate what we already had, not what we wanted. Always say please and thank you. In fact, being humble is sometimes associated with politeness and being kind. Not only are these traits we would all like to possess, but we tend to surround ourselves with people who demonstrate these ideals. Who wants to be around someone who is constantly talking about themselves, bragging about how good they are? You know, the "I, I, Me, Me" people, the kind who speak mostly about their own feats and accomplishments. They tend to dominate the conversation, even when you have a chance to add to it. These can be a few of the many ways to identify someone with a large ego, which is an essential skill when you engage in a meeting.

We discussed earlier how great communicators listen and ask about the person they are conversing with, and don't jump into the discussion trying to dominate the conversation. In fact, accomplishing this takes an ego within yourself not to invade someone's conversation, because it can prove valuable to sit back and gather worthwhile information about someone, rather than talk about yourself. At the same time, your listening skills help feed this person's own ego, as they will enjoy talking about themselves.

> Having an ego can, in fact, be part of our leadership toolbox.

In all the research and reading I have done over the years, I find it strange that most authors discuss how to practice humility when in a leadership role. Many people talk of "no egos."

However, most of the great leaders I have been around have a bit of "swagger" to them. My great mentor and college coach, Bill Holowaty, use to shout during practice, "Ya better have a little piss and vinegar if ya wanna play on our team." He meant that you better have a look in your eye, and a walk in your step, that show confidence, that display an ego.

The people whose stories I share in this book, along with many other successful people in business and in sports, have demonstrated *huge* egos. Yet when I read though many of the leadership guides that are out there, rarely is it discussed that egos are present. Good leaders find a way to have their egos rub off on people they have invited into their organization.

In reality, having an ego can, in fact, be part of our leadership toolbox. However, a quality leader can master the craft of what I call "circling the wagons" when letting egos become present in their own organization.

Crank Up Your Ego—Sometimes

There is a popular belief that being humble will lead to a more cohesive organization, and thus to better teamwork. Some authors describe the importance of humility when trying to establish a good working environment in an organization. Yet where the confusion comes from is that most leaders, at least in my experience, have a strong ego.

How does this work?

Well, I might blow your minds a bit with the rest of this chapter, but I disagree with the "no ego" way of thinking when it comes to leading your team to greatness. Actually, I don't entirely disagree, because there is a time to be humble inside your family, team, or organization.

You actually *need* an ego to be great, to lead your organization and team to success. The people in the organization have to possess the ability to believe in greatness. They need to think, or have been led to think, they were hired and are present within an organization because someone believed not only that they have the ability to be on the team, but that they can be a superstar of that organization. That's why they hired *you*: to be the best. The people brought to a program need to think big—they need to think they are the best.

> You need an ego to be great.

It is rarely taught and many authors are not willing to go down the slippery slope to say this, but you need big egos in order to be successful. A great leader will foster and actually feed the egos of his or her employees. You need an ego to be great.

However, you also need to leave that ego outside when working with your own group. That same leader who fed the individual's egos will know how to temper, and even turn off the ego at appropriate times. These times are when teammates or work colleagues come together to form a program. The employees or team members now get rid of any egos and don't let them into the culture of the program that is developed for long-term success. Teams are usually filled with members who didn't leave egos outside, but allowed them to infiltrate the organization. Programs are full of highly talented and confident people. But they know how to work together, focusing on program values, and they see the importance in everyone pulling in the same direction.

When members walk into the office building each day, their egos needs to be left in the parking lot. This is where humility takes a front seat in the organization. Have humility when interacting with your family, your team, your employees, your business.

Almost every successful person I have been around has, at times, demonstrated a sense of great ego. They believed they were very good at what they do. Also, just as important, they convinced their employees they were great.

How can you expect to win championships, close huge accounts, or compete every day with the opposition if you don't believe you and the people around you can be the best?

But there is a fine line between fueling your own and your group's egos. Think about replacing the word "ego" with "confidence." You certainly don't want the "I, I, Me, Me" type of ego of a loud-mouthed braggart. It's about having a confident swagger. That certain look in your eye and spring in your step that shows you truly know what you are doing. Your ego is present, yet not overtly advertised.

Thinking big is a very important part of building a strong culture and needs to be present in order to do great things—things like winning at the highest level, scoring big accounts for your firm, and even leading the region in corporate sales. This, of course, takes ego to convince yourself and the members of your team that you belong on such a large scale.

> Think big, and believe you have the
> power to do great things every day.

Conversely, you and the people of your organization must lose that same huge ego among yourselves. This can be tricky, because we always need to have internal competition among our team. The ability to compete internally will only make outside competition that much easier. That is why we practice. It is an important part of leadership to fuel the egos of your team when they compete among themselves. However, a critical step is finding when those internal competitions come to an end, practice is over, and now your group is ready to compete with outside organizations. Only at that point do those egos within your team need to disappear. Now the team is working together, pulling for one another to bring success to the organization in external competition.

As a manager and a leader, you have to constantly pay attention to the egos within your organization. You don't want your people to lose them, yet there is a time they need to be reminded to take the "no ego" approach. This is when the group is ready to compete externally, and within their own ranks there needs to be a humble approach. All team members are equal at this point, from the CEO to the first-year salesperson to the person cleaning out the wastebaskets—everyone working together.

Think Big

Whenever I am asked to speak to a group on organizational leadership, I ask them about their egos. For instance, let's say I am speaking to the employees at Darling's Auto dealers in the great state of Maine. At first, most people are very humble and respond that they believe you cannot foster any egos if you want team unity.

Then I ask them: do you want to be the best car dealership in Bangor, Maine? In the State of Maine? How about the Northeast? Why not be the best in the country?

Think big and believe you have the power to do great things every day. I ask them: do you agree? Do you want to be the best in the land?

The audience goes wild. Heads nod in agreement. A lot of people mumble "Yes, sir!" They always get fired up to hear that. Then I bring up the fact you can't ever think this big unless you have the ego to be great. It takes tremendous effort to walk this walk. It takes dedication to the core values of their organization, along with spending daily attention to them.

> Great leaders always send the message
> that everyone within the organization is
> vital and important.

However, what needs to be present is the ability to circle those wagons. Leave the huge ego outside when you are walking into your place of employment, or with your family or team. Great leaders always send the message that everyone within the organization is vital and important.

It gets us back to empowerment leadership. No one is too small to be heard, from a vice president to the person responsible for cleaning the floors. Everyone must feel part of the organization in order to achieve long-term program success. That is where you, as a leader, teach everyone how to circle the organizational wagons.

Circle the Wagons

Remember the old Western movies, when settlers in the 1800s were moving west? These films always showed the trials and tribulations of this difficult journey. Settlers would jam into horse-drawn wagons, packed with all their belongings. Inevitably, there would be a surprise attack by Native Americans, understandably angry that these Easterners were invading their homeland. A turf war would ensue, with arrows and bullets flying.

To defend themselves, the settlers circled their wagons into a moving train, so they could fight from one side of the circle of wagons. Therefore, they only had to defend half of their territory.

Good leaders teach their people how to "circle their wagons." They know how to rally the troops and work together in an efficient and effective manner. Naturally, this means teamwork. With any good program or organization, leaders need to surround themselves with people who have confidence in what they were brought there to accomplish. The team needs to believe, or be led to believe, that they are the best at what they do. Teamwork does, in fact, need everyone in the group to be pulling together, working toward a common goal. But they must possess an ego that they will accomplish great things because they are part of the best team. So, as a leader, circling your wagons with confident, audacious individuals is essential to leading them to a successful outcome.

Invest in Values

However, it can be quite difficult to foster an environment of egoless people internally. Finding a way to balance the egos that come with motivated employees can certainly backfire if you are not willing to invest your time in the values that make up the strong culture of your organization.

Let me give you an example about egos on a college baseball team. We recruit, hopefully, the best young players in the country, players who are drafted by major-league teams out of high school, yet defer their professional career a few years to attend college. Every fall, a few talented ballplayers walk through our locker room door, ready to embark on their college careers. Most of them have been the best player on the teams they have been a part of all their lives. They have not only been told that, but they have proven it with their play. And, like clockwork, these freshmen players walk into our family of returning players and start to talk the talk.

Their huge ego comes out. "Hey Jorgie, I know you started every game last year as shortstop, but get ready to lose your job."

Now, we need these talented ballplayers to come into our program and they will undoubtedly bring the physical tools to help us succeed, and foster the internal competition needed to push each individual to work as hard as they are capable of. But what quickly happens in that locker room, if I did my job as their leader, is that the returning players start the process of educating our new faces to check that ego in the parking lot. It is certainly difficult to do this; it takes tremendous effort and a focus on the program's values. And some will not make it. They are not willing to buy into our core values. (We will discuss this later on how to recognize the naysayers of an organization who can cost you valuable time and money.)

What is understood is that we need the egos to be present and want everyone to believe they have the capability to be great. That greatness and success will only come if you work hard to buy into the team's culture, and also check that ego when circling the team's wagons.

Another example of possessing an ego, yet checking it at the door when it's for the good of the program, is the 2018 Stetson team. We were navigating through a strong season, with a record of 30–8 and about a quarter of the season remaining. The team had worked hard throughout the year on a strong culture, practicing every day the core values from the "Values Wall" I explained earlier in the book.

We were scheduled to head on a five-game road trip, playing NCAA perennial powerhouse the Florida State Seminoles, then continue on to a conference weekend series against the New Jersey Institute of Technology. Our team had a very talented pitching staff, but pretty average hitters, nothing to blow you away. Yet the players did a great job focusing on their strength of pitching well and playing good defense, then trying to find ways to score a few runs. From the start of the season, they believed they were the best, Omaha bound. (This is a term used when an NCAA Division I team qualifies for the College World Series, which is held in Omaha, Nebraska.)

This group had tremendous egos. We all fueled them each day, not only talking about Omaha, but instilling the values it would take to be better than our competition, every day. Yet, this group would turn off their egos when around each other.

In baseball, sometimes these egos come out not only in the clubhouse, but on the field of play. For instance, there is a great example of how egos present in the game can be detrimental. When a coach makes out a lineup and shuffles the players, 1 through 9, you try to get your best hitters at the top, in hopes they come more often. And you usually put your best hitters at number 3 and 4, so hitters 1 and 2 are on base, therefore allowing them to drive in the runs with a base hit to the outfield.

To understand this story, you need to understand "bunting" the baseball. Bunting a ball is achieved when instead of fully swinging the bat, the hitter waits until the last possible moment, when the ball is out of the pitcher's hand and on the way, to try to "dink" the ball in the direction of a first or third basemen. This forces the defensive infielder to run in and field a slow, weak ground ball. Bunting is usually left to the small, quick hitters in the number 8, 9, 1, and 2 hitting spots in the lineup, certainly not the 3 and 4 hitters. You might even get heckled by the other team if you bunt when the number 3 or 4 hitter is up to bat. And if a coach asks those middle-of-the-lineup hitters to bunt, their ego may surface and they may question the coach about why they've been asked to bunt.

As I said, that 2018 team had some tremendous egos, truly believing they were the best in the nation. But they had the ability to check those egos. The leader of that team, and captain, was a player named Brooks Wilson, whom I first mentioned in Chapter 11. Brooks was one of the best pitchers on the team—the "closer." His job was to come into the game in the last few innings and shut down the other team, to close out the game. And he was good at it. In fact, by the end of this season, he would lead the nation in saves, becoming the best closer in NCAA baseball that year.

Brooksie had one huge ego too. He wore his emotions on his sleeve. Yet he was also the player at the end of that game to pick up every paper cup in the dugout and throw them in the trash and he didn't leave the field until everything was put away. He led by example.

Brooks was also one of the best hitters on the team, the number 4 hitter in the lineup. So you would assume that, with his huge ego, each time he stepped up to the plate to hit, he would try to do the macho thing and hit a home run. Well, Brooks had the ability of a true leader, and could check that ego when it benefited the organization, or in this case the Stetson program. There were plenty of times when there was a runner on third base, 90 feet away from scoring a run, and Brooks was up to bat. Everyone assumed he would try to hit it off or over the outfield fence. But Brooks would take a peek at how deep the third baseman was playing, and if he caught him sleeping and playing too deep, the ego of a typical number 4 hitter would go out the window. Good ole Brooksie would lay down a perfect bunt, allowing the run to score, with him taking the infield single. If he was ever questioned, his answer was simple: "Why swing for the fences when I can help the team win in other ways?"

No ego present. Brooksie did what was best for the program, not for Brooks.

Build the Team's Confidence

Why is ego so important to observe, as a leader within your organization? By now, you are most likely thinking I am telling you to get a bunch of cocky, arrogant employees together and all will be great.

Well, that's not exactly where I am going and it's much harder than that. As you guide your group to invest in core values, you need to continually watch for a positive culture. You need to pay extreme attention to the members of the organization and how they interact with one another. Having an ego that exists outside the group ultimately gets them to build confidence and not arrogance. Confidence they can tackle projects, tasks, and even conquer opponents. The number one thing I find in organizations is employees' lack of confidence. When you, as a supervisor, help the people of your organization believe in themselves, grow their ego, and build that grit, they become more and more confident. The more confident they are, the more they communicate.

Confidence strengthens communication.

FIGURE 13.1   Must-have components to achieve the win.

We spent an entire chapter earlier discussing the importance of being a strong communicator. It is human nature that the more confident you are in something, the more likely you are to communicate your thoughts and ideas. Once a person is confident and can communicate effectively, it ultimately drives them to compete. Confidence builds communication skills. Communication leads to preparedness to compete. Being prepared to compete give you a better chance to *win* (see Figure 13.1).

Tone People Down, Not Up

If you can develop a strong culture within your organization, you have the ability to foster the cultural environment where egos can, in fact, be present. Remember, strong values lead to a culture that gives you the flexibility to step outside the organizations' comfort zone of "no egos," as your employees know these values you expect they possess.

Another way to think of this is that in order to be a great organization, the leader needs to work on toning people down, not toning them up. If you are constantly trying to motivate team members to go, go, go, instead of pumping the breaks, it takes much more time and energy. People who have the will to "grind" and the inner drive to succeed are the ones you need to have on your team or organization. Finding those individuals during the hiring or recruiting process when you are forming your team is an essential step. You want highly motivated people, maybe even too motivated. Your role as their leader is to understand when to let them go and spread their wings, along with when to reel them back in if they get a bit out of control.

Let me give you another baseball example of what I mean. When I recruit ballplayers, I obviously want talented people who bring a bit of swagger and energy. Now, envision a close game against a rival team, and it's coming down to the ninth inning. Do I want to look down the dugout, only to see the players sitting down on the bench, looking disinterested and not cheering on their teammates on the field? Or do I want to see a bunch of crazy guys, cheering and going nuts, to the point where fans and the other team are wondering what is going on? Well, sometimes that crazy dugout goes a bit too far, and crosses an invisible line. They might yell a choice word, or direct a comment at an opponent. So, as their supervisor, I have to quell that and tone them down a bit.

"Fellas, I love the excitement, but keep it clean and with us!"

When you create a strong culture, coupled with surrounding yourself with strong people, your group becomes driven to reach any goals you might set. The people of the organization you put together will be fueled and pushed to reach these goals by the challenges, competition, and beliefs that arise each day.

Stubbornness Can Be a Good Trait

Sometimes employees' egos are accompanied by a bit of stubbornness, and occasionally you have to tone it down.

Can stubbornness be a good thing?

At first glance, stubbornness is generally viewed as a negative. However, with the proper guidance and attention to core values from the leader, it can drive this personality trait to channel any stubbornness to a path of success. The will to succeed becomes more and more present, and a group of motivated individuals within an organization will come together to achieve many of the goals set.

Now, back to that Stetson baseball road trip to FSU and NJIT. The 2018 Stetson baseball team did not play well one particular week, losing two games to Florida State. In the next three-game series with NJIT, the first two were successful in terms of the outcome, but the team did not play well. Game three handed us a loss, the first loss to NJIT in Stetson's history. As the team traveled back to Florida, players were pretty silent. They were very emotional. Mad. Embarrassed. Their big egos took a dent.

Upon returning to Stetson, I called a team meeting in hopes of getting them back on track and shifting their focus on the process of moving forward in the face of failure.

> His attitude became contagious with the
> rest of the team.

In fact, deep down inside, I was a bit happy that the three losses had happened. Up to this point, the team had very little failure. If I did my job as the leader, I had a chance to let these setbacks guide the team and help them to reach long-term success. In our meeting, we discussed how to build off our failures and learn from what we did wrong. Then something happened I will never forget. This group of players, this *team*, became really stubborn.

One member, Jack Perkins, stood up and calmly said, "We are not gonna lose again, plain and simple. And Coach, we are not just saying this—we mean it. Guys, whatever we have done up until today is history. But we also need to work way harder if we want to do what we say, and that is go to Omaha."

Jack was very stubborn that day, and his attitude became contagious with the rest of the team. For the remaining days of the 2018 season, I witnessed this group doing more and more. Practicing harder, focusing more, even picking up cups in the dugout together. After that team meeting, this team reeled off 18 wins in a row, leading Division I baseball in the longest winning streak that season, and the longest in Stetson history. They went on to a record of 48–13, one game shy of reaching Omaha. Ironically, Brooks Wilson was at the plate up to bat in that final game, with two out, and two runners on base. The score was 7–5 with Stetson losing. Brooks hit a ball to the deepest part of the ballpark, only to have the ball caught by the center fielder, as he leaped at the fence, five feet short of a walk-off win. When that last out was made, the team knew the historic season had ended.

After a few minutes, I met with the group after the emotions of a tough loss subsided. I explained what a great run, a historic run, this team had had, and how proud the Stetson community was. In fact, they became the darlings of college baseball in the later weeks of the 2018 season. I hoped they could take a deep breath and cherish the success they accomplished.

But that stubbornness this team possessed showed up again. They were pissed. Really mad. They wanted more. There was no talking to them right then and there. I had no pep talk or words of encouragement to ease their emotions. They didn't want to leave the field. They wanted to start the next season that day! Their desire to prove to themselves from their setback and failures outweighed the mindset to celebrate. They were a driven bunch, full of ego and stubbornness because their season had ended, and they wanted more.

So, as you can see, it is okay to have egos. And with that, stubbornness can also be present in a positive manner. This is where the leader of an organization needs to shine. If he or she is not willing to invest in the time and energy it takes to establish, adjust, and pivot with the core values, these egos can lead to fractures within the organization.

Fostering egos within your organization can be useful. These egos allow confidence to flow, leading to better communication when trying to win that huge account or a baseball game against the competitors. A leader must embrace the inherent power of the ego as a tool in the toolbox. But remember that with great egos comes great responsibility to drive home the core values you establish within your organization—values such as teamwork, communication, image, and attitude. So you need to surround yourself with some egos, but work to create an egoless environment within your own house!

Coach's Challenge

1. What are some positive ways you can best use your own ego within your organization?
2. How do you practice checking your own ego when dealing with your team?
3. How can you recognize positive stubbornness?
4. How do egos and stubbornness hinder your path to being a good leader? To organizational success?

14

The Art of Decompression

A common dominator that leaders have built into their DNA is to have the ability to follow many of the traits and core values they believe in, with great vigor, on a consistent basis. Yet, when you invest time, energy, and money, the personal sacrifice can be stressful, especially for those whose personality puts added pressure on themselves.

Most successful people operate at a high level of energy, focus, determination, and persistence. Those with high-level energy have a tendency to be hyper-focused on the task at hand, making sure they are prepared, even overprepared at times. A strong leader's energy flame burns fast and hot! And flames need fuel to keep going. That's why prolific leaders seek out "fuel" in terms of education, experience, praise, and success.

All this can take a physical and mental toll on an individual. Research shows the dangers on one's health from stress in the workplace. The rigors of business travel, sales meetings, rejection, dissatisfied customers, hiring and firing employees, and many other day-to-day events can mount up and wear a person down.

High-level achievers need the ability to decompress, to take a mental break and allow the senses to focus on something completely unrelated to the work environment. Thus, when they return to the workplace, they feel reenergized and ready to jump back into the corporate world at full capacity.

Recharge Your Batteries

Just as your body needs refueling with proper nutrition, so does your mind. Finding an outlet to recharge your batteries allows you to get back in the fight with newfound energy and enthusiasm. Yet this form of fuel is underappreciated and seldom discussed because it contradicts the image employees want to project through hard work and the grinder mentality.

Too many times people fail to take a break, go on vacation, or even push back from their desk for a moment to clear their minds. Many people allow stress to perpetuate, resulting in poor health and reduced mental wellness. Without an outlet, many will eventually experience work burnout.

I know this sounds morbid, but take a moment to imagine yourself lying on your deathbed. What do you want to be remembered for and what memories do you want to have at that moment? Are you thinking about a major account you were responsible for closing 40 years ago, or about that week away from work to spend with your family at the beach when your kids were still in diapers? Which one is more important?

If you work hard, you also need to take the time to relax and smell those roses in your personal life. If you truly invest in your organization, people will recognize your efforts. Allow your actions and effort to speak for themselves.

It is vital for successful leaders to decompress for their longevity and well-being. A round of golf with a buddy, a brisk walk, or a yoga class can be a simple mind-clearing activity. Or a week-long family vacation at the beach can recharge your batteries. Maybe you love to travel or even take on a project from somewhere other than your work environment. Whatever your hobby or passion outside the workplace, you must indulge in it to get refocused on work once you check back in.

You've Earned a Break

Many people overlook this essential piece of leadership because they view it as not working hard enough and not finishing a work week, month, or year. I call BS on that, because if you are engaged in a highly competitive environment, working your tail off, week after week, no human being can sustain that level of intensity indefinitely. You have to be able to tell yourself, "You earned this hiatus!"

On the other hand, those who operate at a 50 percent pace throughout the day, only to look forward to a break are the employees whom you, as a supervisor, need to be aware of. Are those individuals the ones you want on your team? Do they have the work ethic and intensity you seek?

It is much better to have employees able to put in 100 percent effort, 50 percent of the time, as opposed to someone working 50 percent effort, 100 percent of the time. In order to put in maximum effort with great energy, you need to be fresh and locked in. Decompression is necessary to achieve this.

People should not feel guilty for taking personal time to rejuvenate and recharge. You, as a leader, need to encourage your staff, co-workers, and teammates to take time away from the workplace and practice self-care in order to return to work healthier and more motivated. The recharge you are asking your team to be mindful of is a step in the process of long-term success within your organization.

> The recharge you are asking your team to be mindful of is a step in the process of long-term success within your organization.

Hone Your Focus Skill

Most successful people have the ability to really lock into a job, investing all their experience and dedication in a particular task. They develop an "all in" mentality to complete a task or project. They become very focused to get the job done.

When you find yourself getting distracted or experiencing burnout, the first step is recognizing that it is time to pivot and take a break. Recalibration can help clear your mind. When you discover the importance of decompression, only then can you master the skill of focus.

> Decompression actually allows you to become better equipped when having to focus and refocus.

If you don't take the time to decompress. a vicious cycle can occur. You want to work harder than others to prove you can get the job done, believing a break will show weakness or laziness. But when you get to the burnout stage in trying to complete the task, your work suffers because you aren't as focused or locked in. Decompression actually allows you to become better equipped when having to focus and refocus.

This skill needs to be practiced, just like any other. You must gain the ability to mentally remove yourself from one situation, and channel all your energy and thoughts to the outlet—the decompression—you choose. It's counterproductive if you leave the office early after an intense meeting to take a brisk walk or meet up with friend to attend a matinee and don't take your mind off that meeting. This is not easy—guilty thoughts continue to run through your mind. I struggle with this exact thing all the time.

How can I take time off to go to the beach? Recruits have to be called, buses and trips have to be scheduled, and money has to be raised for our continued success. Guess what? Those tasks are always going to be there. But if I get burnt out from doing these things during my workday, I certainly won't last long. Worse still, I won't be in the right frame of mind when it is go time and I have to lead my team, co-workers, and organization. I won't be able to give 100 percent if I am not focused and dedicated to the tasks at hand.

Additionally, decompressing gives you a great chance to trust the people around you. What better way to empower your assistants and employees than to let them know you will be headed out for a few days and send the message that you have all the faith in the world they will not only keep the corporate ship straight, but advance it in many ways!

I mentioned earlier that I am an avid hunter and have grown to appreciate being in the woods, not always with the intention of harvesting a deer, but to enjoy the surroundings and use the time to sharpen my senses. Many times, after a grueling work week, I found it a useful outlet to take a walk in the woods, with no thought of even seeing a whitetail.

Rather, I would trek to the backwoods of rural Maine, hiking for hours through swamps and snow, just to be one with nature. I would park my truck prior to sun up, well before most people were starting their morning. Once I found a clearing, I would plop down with my back against a tree. I especially enjoyed when there was no wind blowing and the sun was coming up, glistening off the snow. Once I was comfortably settled in and my heart rate had decreased after the strenuous walk, I found my senses became heightened. I learned to practice the art of focusing with intensity. I would see a branch move slightly from over 100 yards away, only to see a bird fly off it moments later. A simple snap of a stick behind me would turn out to be a squirrel jumping from log to log. Leaves would rustle a long way, making me believe a moose was approaching, only to see a rabbit pop into view.

The more I focused on the nature that surrounded me, the more I forgot about the issues back at the office. I reset my mind, and always left the woods feeling energized. It meant I could return to my job with a newfound sense of focus and vitality. I developed the knack of transitioning my focus from situation to situation. It taught me to lock in to what I am currently engaged with, allowing me to be better prepared for any issues when they arise. Strengthening my focus and attentiveness makes me better equipped to manage critical decisions and situations that surface when in a leadership role.

Lock In

Learning how to focus on a task at hand is something that can be practiced and will prove to be a necessary trait as you grow in your leadership role. A term often used to describe a high concentration level is "locked in."

"That basketball player was laser focused and locked in at the free throw line, allowing her to knock down 10 shots in a row."

"Lisa, you did a tremendous job with your presentation to the board of trustees this morning. You had the crowd locked in."

To "lock in" and perform at a high level is yet another essential trait of an effective and influential leader, both in business and in sport. Leaders don't allow surrounding distractions, noise, or even chaos to derail them. In fact, most leaders actually thrive in environments where distractions exist. They have a high level of concentration, yet recognize when they lose focus. They can step out of the task for a moment, refocus, and return to the assignment. This level of commitment to focusing and locking in ultimately sharpens one's mind.

> Leaders find outlets away from the intense workload to lose themselves and decompress, allowing their minds to reset.

A large part of why great leaders can be successful at focusing is that they are prepared for what they are currently working on. Because they did their best to prepare, along with running any foreseeable obstacles that might occur, they don't feel added pressure. They prepare for a smooth outcome, and for crisis management. They find outlets away from the intense workload to lose themselves and decompress, allowing their minds to reset. The leaders can perform at a higher level of competence under the pressures that exist within the workplace because they've taken the time to recharge. In addition, they know they will have an opportunity to recharge in the near future once a particular work task is complete. It actually acts as a carrot dangling in front of their face, and their focus can lead to the reward of a well-earned decompression.

Burn Those Lines in the Grass

Let me give you an example of how this has worked for me. When I was in college, my summer job was cutting lawns. I really wanted to be good at it and impress my boss and the customers. So I learned how to stripe lawns in intricate and eye-catching mowing patterns, like those patterns you see on the field when watching a baseball game. Like the grass lines on the cover of this book!

When the lawnmower cuts the grass, it lays each individual blade in a certain direction. Each blade has a light-shaded and a dark-shaded side to it. The more times you cut your line in one direction, the "brighter" the line becomes. When you turn to do the next line, you notice the line you just cut is now dark, because the darker side is lying in that direction. The landscapers at golf courses and ballfields just happen to cut those lines multiple times a day, sort of "burning" those lines into the grass.

I wanted to stripe my customers' lawns, so I made a point to take my time, focus on being straight with my first cut, and then repeat the same pattern. Although it took double the time to cut everyone's lawn, my boss heard rave reviews. His phone began to ring from neighbors wanting to switch to our company. He had to hire more guys, but we had to train them to focus on cutting straight lines, otherwise I would have to spend my time fixing their work.

Later in life, as I entered the coaching world, I did my best to work hard and put every ounce of energy into my job and the school I worked for. I found myself losing focus at times and needed to take that mental break. But I didn't have a ton of hobbies, outside of a good walk while hunting. Golf was fun, but took up a lot of my time with little results. Fishing could work, but I didn't want to invest in a boat.

So I cut grass. I would jump on my lawn mower and stripe my lawn. My neighbors all thought I was nuts, cutting for hours upon end. Many times I would get inventive and burn in squiggly lines, or even a checkerboard design. Cutting grass became my outlet; if I didn't fully focus on keeping my mower straight, doubling and even tripling up my mowing pattern, the end product would suffer. After I finished, I felt satisfied with my work, and my mind would be ready to reengage. Heading into the office the next morning, I made sure that as I stepped out of my car, I was locked in for the day's challenges and rewards. I had found a way to practice the ability to lock in.

Find Something You're Good at and Use It as Your Outlet

A key point to notice is that most leaders do find an outlet to concentrate on, freeing up their minds and reenergizing for a later return to the workplace. Most will gravitate to a hobby or outlet they not only enjoy, but are somewhat good at. A hobby of your choosing tends to elicit personal gratification.

If you never played tennis before and you decide this will be your new outlet, you may discover it is harder than it looks, and you likely will not stick with it for very long. Before entirely throwing in the towel, you might take a lesson or two. When the skills you were taught don't translate into results, you become frustrated. When frustration sets in, your mind wanders to things other than your outlet. Thus the tennis lesson fails to improve your game, and frustration, lack of confidence, and disinterest will set in. So much for your new outlet!

When the focus to improve and learn is absent, you miss the opportunity to practice the skill to lock in to the task you are currently engaged with.

Find whatever piques your interest and
take time to decompress.

This is why it is sometimes difficult to find an outlet. This is also why some people have a tough time advancing in their respected field of work. Some may question if the profession they chose is what they truly enjoy, one that will allow them to grow and lead. Hopefully, everyone has the chance to be in a position in which they enjoy not only the work, but also the people around them. This contributes to finding ways to become a better leader to their co-workers, and to bring a positive influence to the organization or team.

Pick an outlet and stick with it for a while. Look for small improvements and growth. Find ways to hone the skill to lock in.

Some people choose to exercise while others engage in hobbies like fishing, reading, or gardening. My recommendation is to find whatever piques your interest and take time to decompress, because this can be an important tool as you build strong and reliable leadership skills.

Honing your senses, to allow yourself to focus and refocus, is something that is extremely important. Decompressing from work, finding that one outlet to take you away from the rigors and stresses that come when leading a group, can pay dividends when you reengage your work environment.

Coach's Challenge

1. What is one of your favorite outlets, one that you can really "lose" yourself in?"
2. Think of a way you can decompress with your family.
3. Make a point to empower others in your organization when you take time to decompress.
4. Challenge yourself to lock in to small moments throughout the day.

15

Winners versus Losers

Whether in sport or business, most people consider winning as *success* and losing as *failure*, which has some truth to it. However, as we discussed earlier, failure can be a path to success, as long as we keep a positive perspective on negative outcomes. So some losing situations can lead to long-term wins.

I have experienced both winning and losing in sports and in life. It took me a period of time early in my professional career to figure out that those loses were pathways to future success. Through my reflections and analysis, I have determined certain traits that stand out to define winners and losers. I have also found that in today's society, people are uncomfortable with the term "loser." The softer way to discuss it is "successes" versus "setbacks."

Well, sorry folks, I won't sugarcoat it. Many people are afraid to hurt feelings and would rather use a hug than a kick in the butt.

I believe that a true leader will teach in many ways; sometimes that takes a hug, and sometimes a push. What follows is how I help my teams replicate their wins and deal with their losses.

Team versus Program

Winning programs and organizations—stable, consistent ones— have people who consistently demonstrate a "winning mentality."

Let me explain the difference between a "team" and a "program." Teams are built for the short term. Coaches at the professional and college levels recruit or sign players with talent, but they are not concerned with building a foundation of long-term success. Businesses bring in the dictator CEO we spoke of earlier to use tactics to show short-term gains.

Programs are built to sustain a level of success that is consistent year after year. It is quite difficult to "win" every year, in both sports and business. However, winning programs create a stable environment and culture that enables them to be in position to compete for wins, championships, and success each year.

Think of sports teams like the New England Patriots or the UCLA Bruins under Coach John Wooden. It is evident they have a formula of *program* success. They consistently speak of team-oriented goals and processes and have an uncanny ability to find players whom no one else wants and make them into not only useful participants, but high-level contributors. There is a clear winning culture that their leaders work extremely hard to maintain.

A common denominator is consistency. They stay consistent to their core values, and no one person is greater than the sum of the organization. They clearly have respect and serve each component of the organization in a way they feel part of the success. No superstar is brought in to change this. In fact, quite the contrary. Many times they take a superstar who was a culture wrecker in one organization and infuse them into their culture. Prior to their arrival that player is informed that, if they join them, there will be no accessions to their previous behavior. It doesn't always work, but they have proven more times than not that it has. They are consistent with their values to all.

If you observe the many successful businesses that also demonstrate a winning program mentality, you will see a clear parallel. All of their players, employees, and the entire organization engage in a winning, competitive environment.

True Toughness

We spoke earlier about competing every day and how valuable that can be for an organization. Winners know the importance of competition. They embrace it. They certainly hate to lose, but they also know that losses will inevitably happen and can be done with grace. Losses are also a path to future success, because the true winner knows how to learn from these losses. They adapt. Adjust. Our compete level can define us as winners or losers.

These traits are not values—don't get that confused. Values are a set of beliefs, both written and unwritten, that you and your organization invest in each day. They define who we are as a group and what we strive for. Traits are tendencies we look for to see if an individual has the capacity to share in these values.

In my final few years at UMaine, Bob Walsh was hired as the men's basketball coach. I had been with the Black Bears as the baseball coach the previous eight years and was at the stage of my career where I was absorbing everything I could in terms of leadership. Bob had tremendous success at the NCAA Division 3 level of coaching, with many championship seasons under his belt. He was excited to get his first go at a DI program, and had tons of energy and passion for coaching.

As with any organization, there are little ways you learn to navigate daily life in order to make things easier. Since I was a veteran there, I surely wanted to help Bob out in the first months with day-to-day issues I had experience with, from filling out the proper paperwork for purchasing equipment, to how we shared weight room facilities between teams.

Our relationship began to grow, and we started to share coaching theories and teaching moments. I couldn't tell you the first thing about running a basketball play or a certain defense to teach, but Bob was a lifelong baseball fan. We began to share our ideas about strong programs, and how culture is key to any organization. The winning teams he had at his previous school had that ingredient, and he did a great job fostering a positive yet competitive environment. He built a winning "program."

One thing we constantly discussed was the ever-changing world of recruiting players. We often spoke of recruiting the "tough" kid, labeled as a "blue-collar" worker. These types, along with those known as "culture kids," are the ones we believed to be the most coachable. These are the recruits, or the employees, who have a positive impact on the culture that we, as leaders, strive to create. They are willing to follow the core values that are established and advocate for others to do the same.

We both agreed that society has changed, and it will always be evolving. The kids of today were finding more excuses for failure, looking to point fingers. I chuckled at times when Bob and I had this discussion; I began to feel like the two old men sitting on the porch of a general store in Maine, sharing coffee and stories of yesteryear. "Back in the day, my coach made me run until I barfed, and I loved it!" And how a coach wouldn't dare to do that today, for fear of losing his or her job.

I found it interesting that Bob and I were talking about toughness, both physical and mental, yet we were also sharing ideas of how to get our message across without offending someone. For instance, we both agreed on the importance of competing, toughness, and an outcome. Whether positive or negative, this outcome will produce a result that you, as a leader, will be able to use to help guide your organization to long-term success. A win in a game needs to be celebrated to foster the addictive nature to want to do it again. A win also needs to be studied in order to see what worked and how to improve, even if the opponent or environment changes.

> A win needs to be celebrated to create the
> addictive nature and want to do it again.

A loss needs to be addressed, corrected, and used to show any weaknesses that can be turned around. A loss can also be hurtful, and one hopes the emotional feeling can motivate the organization to change the outcome in the future.

Winners and Losers

There are still "winners" and "losers" in today's world. Perhaps I should use a bit "softer" term to avoid offending anyone, but the reality is that someone is going to win the account and someone will lose it. People are promoted and fired every day. Yet, remember the simple but powerful message we spoke about earlier, that, used correctly, losing can be a great motivator.

> Losing can be the best motivator if the
> individual—or the organization as a
> whole—has the correct mindset.

Bob shared a few ideas that led me to create a "winning" and "losing" mentality list of traits I look for and certainly mention whenever I speak to an organization about success. And yes, I use the word "loser" in this context to show the motivational factor of failure.

Winning Mentality

Here is a list of little things that I look for when evaluating people to surround myself with. Not all apply all the time, and I encourage you to make your own list of traits you feel are important to you.

- Tries hard not to show fatigue; always has positive body language; does not show the "Monday morning blues"
- First one to arrive and last to leave
- Constantly communicates
- Dislikes "bad" days of work or practice
- Uses words like "my bad" when things don't necessarily go as planned
- Takes responsibility even when it is not their fault
- Is capable of a positive attitude in uncomfortable situations
- Embraces criticism during meetings
- Always aware of their surroundings, and pays attention to the company's image
- Thinks *big* but can focus on the little things each day
- Understands that if program or organizational goals are met, chances of individual success are greater

Losing Mentality

Let's counter the list of winning traits with those that can negatively impact your organization. This can sometimes be challenging, because some of the "superstars" who have the talent others do not possess may also carry these negative traits. It's tempting to believe you can mold these individuals, but I caution you that it's difficult to break these traits. Also, they can have a negative impact on others within our program, which is a "disease" that can spread.

- Makes sure everyone sees how "hard" they are working
- Shows fatigue to let others know they are tired
- Looks for sympathy and comfort from others
- Is frequently in the training room when not injured
- Reacts to negative outcomes with bad body language
- Blames teammates, co-workers, weather, officials, and others for failures
- Finishes sprints in the middle of the pack, but wins the last one
- Puts personal goals in front of the organization
- Counts down on a calendar visiable to others the days to the weekend, vacation or retirement

* * *

Explore how your own list of winning versus losing mentalities can help guide you when building your program. Remember, it is rare to find someone with all the desired traits. You, as the leader, have to create an environment to foster these when you recognize someone is not on the plan you create.

Compete, Compete, Compete

The winning traits we create from a list allow people to establish one key value that rarely is mentioned: the ability to compete. People must know how to establish grit, to fight, to develop a never-give-up attitude and the power to press on through the muck. That is competing.

This is easy to see in sports, which usually involves an athlete locked in, playing hard with physical and mental effort. Yet it also happens in the workforce every day. You have to compete internally with your group, which is vital to the life or death of an organization. You *must* compete on your own team, and the competition needs to be real, with outcomes. There will be winners and losers. Someone is getting a promotion over another. Your job as a leader is to make it fair and positive, and any setbacks or failures an individual experiences are not meant to be career ending. You may have lost today, but you still have a chance to change your role tomorrow.

> You may have lost today, but you still have a chance to change your role tomorrow.

These failures are great roads to future success. Fostering that idea allows people to move forward, and also encourages them not to want to give up too easily on being on top. Once you smell the roses, you usually want more roses. This internal competition also makes outside competition easier. Your program or organization will grow and contend with your counterparts, competing for the sale, account, or win.

Another key factor to realize as a leader is that the people you surround yourself with must either embrace or inherit these traits when you hire or recruit. It is your job to foster the winning mentality.

Most look for the easier path and believe that talent alone can get you to the promised land. We see this both in professional sports and in business all the time. A professional team will "buy up" talent as they head into the playoffs, making trades with players. They give up multiple young, talented kids at the minor league level through a trade to a team that has an older veteran. The veteran can bring value in the short term, but teams have to be careful when bringing new faces into an already successful environment. In business, organizations constantly hire a person to come "shake" things up. The leader and the individual who has succeeded before both hope the infusion of this new employee into the organization can drive others to achieve.

> Talent alone does not allow us to create a
> winning team. You need a strong culture.

As I said earlier, there is great value in hiring people with talent in your field. You do need the horses to pull the cart. But talent alone does not allow us to create a winning team, a winning year, or a winning quarter of earnings. It does not allow us to sustain long-term success. Some of the most talented teams ever assembled could not achieve greatness. We hear it all the time when a group underachieves: "They had all that talent and got beat by a lesser team." Or "That group we assembled never gelled." Talent has nothing to do with culture. Highly skilled employees give you the resources to build something great, something long term. However, it is our responsibility as leaders to advance the group of employees and team members, constantly working on a winning mentality. Ultimately, a strong culture within the organization forms.

So seek to create a *trait* list. What do you look for in your employees in terms of being "winners"? It is vital for you to recognize these winning traits when surrounding yourself with the employees and people you can move forward when forming your team.

Coach's Challenge

1. In the context we just described, are you currently part of a "team" or a "program"?
2. List four traits that best describe "toughness" to you.
3. What are your winning traits? Losing ones?
4. Can you find ways within your organization to compete internally?

16

The 5 Percent Rule

The sum of the group is greater than the individuals.

We've all heard about teamwork and the benefits it can bring to any organization or team. But what is real teamwork? Practicing our trade? Working together for a common goal? Absolutely. Yet so many times a person will not be on the same page inside an organization and will cause issues with a group moving forward. And what is most difficult is having the group focus on improvement each and every day, even when things are going great.

This is where the best teams and organizations shine. They figure out how to improve even when they're on top. It takes great leadership and motivation to drive the group each day. We see it in the best of sports teams and businesses. Bill Belichick has figured this out with the New England Patriots. So did John Wooden at UCLA basketball back in the 1960 and '70s. How about Apple? Walmart? Oprah? All continue to thrive, even as they are on top.

They have found a way to live by the 5 percent rule.

Be Better Every Day

Whenever I speak to a group, I talk about the 5 percent rule. Without it, it is difficult to keep advancing your organization. What is this valuable tool? In order to sustain long-term success, year in and out, you have to find a way to motivate your employees and players to get a little better each week. It seems like a simple task, yet a good leader pays great attention to guiding his or her employees to do the "little" things necessary to grow in small ways, to grow 5 percent in a week.

> Find a way to motivate your employees and players to get a little better each week.

Find a way to be 5 percent better. We spoke in Chapter 15 about the difference between "teams" and "programs." Another winning trait of a program is the ability to have each individual be 5 percent better after each week, which will grow the organization in large ways. Teams consist of individuals who will engage in getting better each week, yet that effort is not intended for the organization's growth, but for individual gains. Again, the sum of our organization can surely be greater than the individuals. Each person's 5 percent effort in a given week, when added to everyone else's effort, can add up and lead to huge gains. I have found that motivating people within an organization can be quite easy when you first set out, as a leader, to show results.

Naturally, practicing longer, providing more training, and working an extra few hours in the week can lead to initial increase in production, especially when everyone in the organization is on board with the 5 percent rule. What proves to be difficult is finding ways to motivate your organization once your group engages in the 5 percent rule for a period of time and has seen the benefits through successful gains. This is where it takes a whole other level of leadership, as we will tackle later in the chapter.

The Power of a Group

I want to share a great story about just how powerful the 5 percent rule can be to an organization. When people on a team or within a group are fully invested to improve not only as individuals but as a group as well, that organization has the ability to grow their core values tenfold.

A few years ago, I was asked by the principal of a middle school to speak to the entire school about leadership and how each student can be a better person. When we sat down to go over the content of the speech I would give, the principal indicated that the students were struggling with communicating and this led to fractures within the classes of grades 6–8. He thought a motivational talk on teamwork and leadership could bring the school closer together. I was happy to see if I could help him build the culture he wanted to bring to his students.

What struck me as odd was his observation about the lack of communication among the students and teachers in the school. It was apparent the lack of communication ran not only student to student, but teacher to student as well. In his view, no one was taking the time to talk, work though problems, and push each other to become better.

It just so happened that my own daughters attended this particular school, and when I quizzed them, they confirmed that many of the students hung out in small groups of friends, never mixing as a large group.

Later that week after I met with the principal, I was able to get everyone together in the auditorium for what I hoped would be a great speech on being a better schoolmate and leader, even at the 13- to 15-year-old level.

I described my 5 percent rule. When you are part of an organization, you have the power to add huge value to the group. The ability to bring a positive outcome to an organization, as one of its members, can be done in many ways, no matter how small or big. Whether it's working later than expected, coming in early, a few extra minutes of studying, or that one extra set of bench presses in the weight room, it's about giving an extra 5 percent effort each day. I use a little saying all the time when I speak to not only my team members, but at every talk I give to organizations: You have to be willing to give your best effort, then give a second effort.

> You have to be willing to give your best
> effort, then give a second effort.

This means 5 percent more, all the time. It can be something as simple as picking up an empty coffee cup from the ground and throwing it in the trash as you enter your workplace. It's probably not in your job description to clean up around the building, but you never know when that next big client is about to walk through the door. Something as small as a piece of trash can affect the entire image of your company, or the school I was about to speak to.

As I began my talk on leadership to the students, I addressed values such as attitude, energy, image, and so on. But I wanted to weave into my talk the value of communicating among the entire school. I came up with a way not only to have them try to communicate more often, but put the 5 percent rule to the test.

I challenged the entire group to be better communicators, and for each one of them to try to be 5 percent better at this for the coming week. There were close to 600 students in the three grade levels at this particular school. I gave a message of just how much impact their group could have if they all tried to be 5 percent better with my challenge, and told them to find the time throughout the day to have a quick conversation with another student or a teacher. Have them ask a simple question of another person to generate quick communication. Where do you live? What's your favorite subject in school? Do you have a pet?

I instructed them to spend the next week, starting the following day, having little chats, at first with someone they knew, then someone they didn't know as well. Huddles was the catchy term we came up with to call our little conversations. Everyone was challenged to have quick huddles throughout the day to engage in better communication.

The students eagerly took my challenge, and I asked them to report back after the week to see how the challenge went. I told them I predicted they would find it awkward at first, but after the ice-breaking period, they would become increasingly confident, along with creating a positive environment within their school.

I found out later that the students fully embraced my challenge and took just a few extra minutes a day to talk with a fellow classmate or a teacher. They witnessed the power of the 5 percent rule. I found it funny when the principal of the school reached out to me again and explained that I caused a bit of a dilemma. The many huddles in between class switches led to late starts each class period! When people in an organization—or in a middle school—do the little things, the gains are immense! These kids proved that by their small individual effort. Everyone has the power to have a huge influence within our organization every day.

It's not always easy to motivate employees and teammates to improve 5 percent each week, but that is where great leaders can share the importance of doing small things to benefit the group. Leaders need to get to know their people and find small ways to push each one, no matter how small, to greatness.

Focus on Small Efforts for Long-Term Success

As with the story about the middle school kids, one thing that happens by practicing the 5 percent rule is the addictive factor that becomes contagious. Remember my discussion about the handshake? When one middle schooler decided to invest in better communication because of the challenge, others followed. One person's attitude can be highly contagious, especially when it is positive and produces positive results. More people within the organization want the same results, and decide to copy what seems to work for others. If you, as the leader, principal, boss, or coach, can motivate your group to strive to be 5 percent better, it undoubtably leads the *program*, not just the team, to long-term success.

But there can be snags. After a period of time when everyone is engaged in the 5 percent rule and gains are made, what's next? How do you find the next way to be 5 percent better? There are only so many extra hours you can put into the workday. You can only volunteer for extra training for so long.

This is where great leaders will constantly find ways to challenge the group to do small tasks that have positive outcomes. The challenges a leader sets can be outside the employees' comfort zone or even not part of their job description. Yet finding small things for the individual to become 5 percent better at will grow the organization on a consistent basis.

Don't neglect to do the little, simple things.

Be great at the things that really should not take a huge effort. Walk into your place of employment each morning and survey the scene, noticing whether the place looks "recruit ready." Can I, as an employee, help the image of our company? Do I leave my desk a mess or can I take an extra few minutes to tidy it up at the end of each day? Can I have a quick conversation with a fellow employee, one I might not know very well, in order to build a better relationship? There are little things that we all can do; we just have to put forth that 5 percent extra effort.

Be Great at Little Things

There is little doubt that developing and sustaining the ability to lead takes effort and energy each and every day. What separates the good leaders from the great ones is when you can still bring leadership traits to your group even when things do not go your way. You have to possess the ability to grind through the muck, because setbacks and failures are inevitable.

> Each person must set examples of being a little better each day, especially at the little things.

Find ways to have a quality routine when things are not going well, along with navigating your organization to improve on things when success does happen. The 5 percent rule allows two important factors to happen. First, it gives everyone a plan to work at the simple traits you and your team value, so when the you-know-what hits the fan, you can refocus. Second, when your group is on top and it seems like nothing can go wrong, it grounds your team a bit, and keeps them focused on the idea that success happened because they took care of the little things.

So, to be a great leader, look at doing 5 percent more each week. Your people will follow, allowing the contagious effect to set in. Great leaders, along with great programs, will be 5 percent better when it goes south or when they are on top of the food chain. They find it easy to be consistent though thick and thin. And we all know that organizations will be on both ends of the success-and-failure spectrum time and time again. The best approach to tip the chart to the positive side for sustainable periods of time is to instill the 5 percent rule.

Coach's Challenge

1. Have you been around someone who works 5 percent harder each day?
2. Find something at your workplace that is not in your job duties to be 5 percent better at, and see if anyone follows your lead.
3. What is a "little thing" you can do for your organization when you feel you are on top?
4. How can you implement the 5 percent rule in your professional and personal life?

17

Shoulda, Woulda, Coulda: Get Rid of It

We previously discussed just how important it is to have a positive attitude, vision, and outlook in order to be a high-quality, long-term successful leader. This trait is even more significant when faced with adversity or failure. It can define whether you, as a leader, are capable of keeping an optimistic view in tough times to lead your people when they need it the most.

However, sometimes the people around you default to negative thoughts. These individuals can have an adverse effect on the culture you worked so hard to build. A leader needs to develop the skills to recognize and address any negative distractions within their organization, yet not become sucked into listening to outside noise from people who want to see you fail. Keep your group on track, and stick to your core values to aid your team's culture.

Shoulda, Woulda, Coulda and the "Negative Nellie"

"I just don't know what to do with Mike. He won't follow any of our rules and is constantly doing the opposite of what I ask him to do. All he does is talk about negative things and say he could do better if he was in charge. He second-guesses every move I make when working with our entire office."

Sound familiar? This is the "Shoulda, woulda, coulda" person in your office or organization, always looking for a reason to doubt. We have all been around this unhappy person. I call them "negative Nellies." "Our supervisor *shoulda* done it this way, not how he said to do it." "If I were in charge, I *woulda* . . ." And of course, "I *coulda* done it so much faster and easier than the way he wants us to." I actually heard this term early in life, and have used it ever since. My high school football coach in New Jersey, Coach Parachuck, constantly repeated this during every practice. "No shoulda, woulda, couldas today—get that out of our team!"

Some things that drive this type of person to such negativity are out of your control as the leader. Home and personal life can affect our ability, and that can be tricky to navigate as a leader. Yet, your overall focus must always circle back to the entire organization, and how you can constantly pay attention to the details you outlined with the group's strong culture.

There are many reasons these people infiltrate the culture you are working hard to achieve. For starters, the amount of time you need to spend dealing with their issues and problems can detract from what you can offer other team members. Your valuable time and energy become focused on one individual instead of the entire group. As we mentioned earlier, culture is ever changing. Just because something worked one week doesn't mean it will always work in the future. Your team and its values need your constant attention. If you, the team leader, has to spend time on this negative Nellie, that takes away from your own goals to lead your organization.

Next, the contagious factor can creep in. We spoke in Chapter 3 of how contagious that handshake can be, and how attitude rubs off on others. That chapter spoke to how a positive attitude will drive others to want to be around that individual, ultimately leading most in the group to be more positive. But the contagious effect can have a damaging outcome as well. The negative person will try to influence others, looking for ways to have a few select people within the organization join their adverse approach, and this then spreads to other team members. When this happens, your job as a leader becomes very difficult.

Move People in the Same Direction

As I stated in the introduction, I didn't come up with a lot of these theories. I was taught these ideas and they continue to work well when implemented them with my own teams. As you navigate through the many principles and styles of leadership, you will find some that fit and some that won't. It is up to you to mesh what you feel comfortable with and have learned into your own leadership portfolio.

One of these leadership principles was shared with me by my friend Bob. Bob owns a large construction company that has grown over the years to employ over 700 workers. He started working for the company many years ago, beginning as a worker on the road crew, learning the business from the bottom up, and climbing the steps of the company ladder. Eventually, he rose to become the president and principle owner, and he has grown it into a leading construction company in his region.

One day, Bob and I went to lunch to discuss me speaking to his company on the topic of teamwork and leadership. Being a big baseball fan, Bob wanted to chat about leadership and see if I could give him some ideas to help his employees work more efficiently and increase production. Over lunch, Bob told me a story where he is constantly on the job sites, making sure guys are showing up—in the right way—and working effectively.

He went on to describe one individual he spent much of his time trying to motivate. This one employee sometimes showed up to the job site either late or hung over. Bob also told me about another individual, this one in an executive role in Bob's leadership team, who would constantly second-guess Bob's supervisors and even Bob himself! Bob noticed other employees starting to act in similar manners. The problem started to become contagious and negatively influence others. Bob also had another dilemma to add to his problems with his current employees. Because there was a shortage of quality workers to hire, it was really difficult to find people to employ. So Bob's problem was not only motivating people to work hard and efficiently, but finding those workers to begin with.

As Bob and I discussed what he might be able to do with his issues, he reached across the table and grabbed a napkin and pen. We began to collaborate, searching for ways to become better leaders when faced with employee issues of negativity. On the napkin, he drew a plus sign, signifying what you sometimes see on a map, like a compass (see Figure 17.1). We then drew two lines, running parallel to the east-west line, both on top of and below the center of our compass.

We discussed that an organization or team is really a large cast of characters that belong to the unit. And on the team

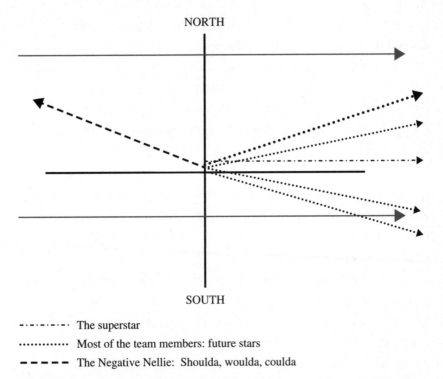

FIGURE 17.1 A typical team or organization when first dealing with a "shoulda, woulda, coulda" person.

there are superstars, future stars, burnt-out stars, and certainly negative Nellies, who aren't really stars at all. They are the "shoulda, woulda, coulda" people.

Bob and I explored ways to lead your people, unit, organization, or team. We used the example of asking the team members to start walking east. Inevitably, the superstar will say "Yes, Sir!" and head out due east. On a team or within an organization, this superstar individual is the starting shortstop, the all-American quarterback, the number one salesperson, or the best lawyer in the firm. We drew a line from near the center of the plus sign straight out to the right, heading east.

Next, we drew a few other lines starting near the center and heading in an easterly direction. They didn't head due east, but they stayed roughly within the two east-west guidelines. We agreed these are the future stars. They represent most of the individuals on Bob's team who might not be the best, but certainly have the capabilities to grow into great teammates and employees. As the leader, Bob needed to focus on these employees, and guide them toward the values he and his company thought were important.

We then drew a line from near the center headed west. This is your negative Nellie (the shoulda, woulda, coulda employee). These were the employees Bob was spending most of his time with, the ones he tried hard just to get to show up to work or to stop second-guessing him.

"Bob, this seems to be one of the realities you struggle with in your company," I explained.

It began to click for Bob that he was never going to get everyone to be a superstar, but should focus on getting everyone going in the same general direction.

We then drew another plus sign on a second napkin. This time, we drew the superstar line in an easterly direction (but not due east) and the future stars were headed north and south (see Figure 17.2). They were well out of the boundaries of the two east-west guidelines from the previous diagram. "Bob, if you spend too much of your valuable time on the negative Nellie line, your others become distracted, causing them to gravitate away from the values and culture you are working so hard to maintain."

What Bob and I were beginning to understand was that although he needed every able body he could get due to the shortage of workers, sometimes the organization suffers when it's filled with shoulda, woulda, coulda, people. Also, when you place the majority of your focus on just a few individual employees, trying to get them to buy into the organization's values and culture,

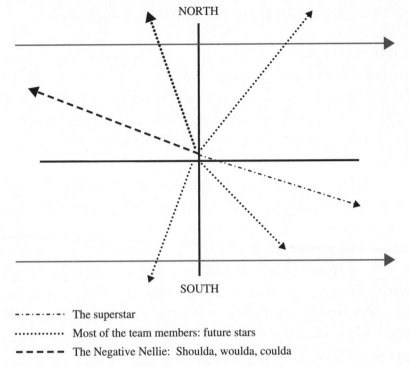

NORTH

SOUTH

- · · — · — · · The superstar
- ············ Most of the team members: future stars
- – – – – The Negative Nellie: Shoulda, woulda, coulda

FIGURE 17.2 What happens to the team when you focus on the "shoulda, woulda, coulda" person.

others will slowly lose their focus on those same principles. It showed Bob that such people can affect his organization, and just how important it is either to turn the negative Nellie around quickly, or get rid of the office malignancy so it doesn't spread and affect others.

Leaders certainly have to make tough decisions. It is why they need to be better prepared every day. When important decisions or crisis management situations are upon them, they must be able to do what is best for their organization. Leaders need to lead the way in these circumstances, and decide if they have the ability to quickly turn a negative employee into a positive, productive one. If not, that individual needs to go.

Neutralizing the Negative Nellie

A common question is: Why do these negative Nellies exist? What drives an individual to be so pessimistic? Inevitably, people just do not want others to succeed. Whether that arises from jealousy, envy, or even spite, there may be people rooting for you to fail as you navigate your organization down the path of a strong culture.

When you find a negative Nellie in your own organization, address the situation swiftly. As leader, one of your roles is to identify anyone on your team who is not on board with your group's culture. Sit down with this individual and communicate how their attitude could be having a negative effect on others. Make it clear you are willing to work with them, invest your own time and energy to aid them to get back on track. Explain how your conversation and their current negative Nellie attitude can be a significant moment to learn and grow.

However, if they are too stubborn to buy in to what you are selling, they will have to go. Such people should no longer be invited to be a part of your organization; they need to be removed before they have a chance to infiltrate further into the program.

"There Is No 'I' in T-E-A-M"

Most people know this famous sports saying, even outside the sports world. The saying arose to show people that, when working as a group toward a common goal, it is important to focus not on being an individual, but a team player.

When I speak to groups, I mention Aristotle's famous phrase: "The whole is greater than the sum of its parts." A single thing made of many separate parts can be more important, more useful, and "greater" than all of the separate parts on their own.

This theory is nothing new, but I also mention something that is rarely practiced: we have to walk the walk when practicing Aristotle's concept. People might believe it is important when leading their organization, but I try to observe how many people, when in a public setting, actually practice what they are preaching. This means you, as a leader, when talking about successes that have been achieved, *never* use the words "I" or "me" when speaking to the group, or about the group to others. We don't want to hear this:

"I thought I did a good job getting the group prepared for the big sales pitch, and was able to lead them to get the client to choose us."

"The game plan I put together today for the defense was perfect, and the hard work put in by me and my assistant allowed the team to be successful."

People who use "I" and "me" are most likely shoulda, woulda, coulda people. They are the ones who blame others for their misfortunes and are always looking for recognition when things go well. They don't practice humility within their own organization and allow their ego to creep into their work family.

We spoke earlier about the importance of having an ego, but remember that it has to be lost in relation to your program, organization, or team. As leaders, we want to use any success as a way to give credit to the team:

"We did a great job today."

"Our entire organization is responsible for the huge account we just nailed today after a stellar sales presentation."

This is hard for most people to do, but you have to make it a practice to avoid the I's and me's whenever possible. Your team will appreciate your "humbleness" in successful situations, because this is a great sign of the empowerment leadership one must instill to aid in the long-term success of the organization.

There *is* one time where "I" and "me" are acceptable to use publicly: when failure, setbacks, or bumps in the road happen within your team. It is another difficult thing for most leaders to do, because the natural reaction is to blame something or someone. Yet, when a supervisor stands before a group and takes responsibility when things don't go as planned, it can lead to a level of loyalty and trust from team members that is otherwise difficult to achieve:

"Today just wasn't our day, folks. I am sorry to announce that after everyone's hard work and preparation for my sales pitch today, we didn't get the account. I did not do a great job in the presentation, and ultimately caused the account to slip by."

In sports, we hear head coaches try this from time to time:

"I did a poor job, as their coach, getting the team ready for our opponent today. I was outcoached and this loss is on me."

Even when the leader might not be directly responsible for the setbacks, he or she owns the failures of the group. In the previous chapter, we discussed what winning and losing can look like, and you should see the value of taking responsibility, even when failure is not your fault.

When you, as a leader, allow your team or organization to take responsibility for the successes, and take the blows yourself for any setbacks, employees become more loyal and begin to trust the supervisor more often than not. When you decide to pass on success and own the setbacks, your organization will grow stronger and aid in the long-term success you and your group strive to achieve.

Coach's Challenge

1. Can you work to eliminate the words "I" and "me?"
2. What tactics can you employ to tackle the negative Nellies in your organization?
3. What can you do better to focus your time and energy on the rising star?
4. Can you learn not to sweat the small stuff? Not worry about the ones who want you to fail?

18

Be a Doer, Not a Talker

I DO. Two powerful words when you stop and think about it, because our minds are constantly telling us to "do" something.

Let's see. I have to do the food shopping, make dinner, get the kids home from practice, meet that deadline for a presentation at work, and so on. We all have daily tasks to accomplish in order to have a functioning work and family life.

As the daily grind of our workday begins, most people get their to-do list going. (My wife calls it the honey-do-list.) It can be scribbled on a yellow sticky note, typed up on the phone, or simply placed on a mental list just after the alarm goes off at 6 a.m. So at 6:01 a.m., a string of obligations runs through our minds: I have to put the garbage out, get the kids fed, walk the dog, and get my big presentation ready for the boss."

We all "do" a lot throughout the course of the day. But what we do are a series of small assignments. Simply put, we follow marching orders set by ourselves or others, in an effort to complete a series of tasks.

What I want to "do" in this chapter is to look at another level of "doing," when you set out to accomplish something much greater than a simple task. This might be something that you are fearful of or that sits completely outside your comfort zone—for example, a project that concerns you because you doubt your abilities to succeed, and it might result in embarrassment, shame, or rejection if not completed properly.

Are you capable of making that leap of faith? Do you have it in you to truly put your head down, buckle that chin strap, and dive head first into something outside your comfort zone? Can you really "grind" out a task or assignment?

We "Do" Our Wedding Vows, Not Just "Say" Them

"I do." We say those two words when we've made the decision to enter into marriage with the love of our life.

"Do you, Mary, take John, to be your husband; promise to be true in good times and in bad, in sickness and in health, with love and honor for all the days of your life?"

"I DO!"

These are very powerful words that come with great responsibility.

"I Do. Forever."

Those who have walked the marriage path likely have amazing memories that last a lifetime. For most people, excitement, fear, nervousness, and joy all lead up to that one special day. Society has taught us that it's a big commitment, that leap of faith we spoke of earlier. So the pressure is there to succeed and not disappoint.

"I don't wanna screw this up." "Am I doing the right thing?"

Uh oh. There goes the confidence, and here comes the second-guessing, those cold feet, that "shoulda, woulda, coulda" talk.

I hope for all, as I did, that you went into that day with an astounding "I DO!" as your mindset. I hope you felt prepared, confident, and so sure of yourself you'd bet the farm on your decision. The person you are marrying is "the one." Those important vows we take on our wedding day are meant to last a lifetime.

If you are fortunate enough to find "the one" and enter into marriage, your wedding day brings great excitement and a bit of tension. You look forward to the ceremony, praying you don't mess up any of the lines you practiced at rehearsal the previous night. Those solemn lines include various commitments to doing: to love and cherish, respect and honor; to laugh and cry together; to care for each other in sickness and in health. You don't just say the words; you commit to doing them.

Can you imagine attending a wedding, only to hear the bride and groom blurt out, "I say" when asked, "Do you . . . ?" Most of the guests would probably think, "Well, that marriage is gonna last all of three weeks."

Would you enter into such a huge, life-changing commitment just by "saying" those important vows? Talking the talk, only to fail to follow through with the commitments you just agreed to? The bride and groom might as well answer their vows with "I guess?" as Grandma falls off her chair and the whole crowd looks on in confusion. It would seem like a skit straight out of *Saturday Night Live*.

Think of an example of "talking" in another way. What if you wake up at 6 a.m. and say you are going to take out the trash, feed the kids breakfast, get them off to school, walk the dog, and then do the shopping. Then you just run the daily list of chores through your head, hit the snooze button, and roll over for a few more hours—it was just "talk." And most likely, chaos would ensue. You would rise from your extended siesta, only to find kids with cereal in their hair, the dog licking up a puddle of milk off the floor, and the school has left messages asking why the kids are absent that day.

Don't Just Talk the Talk

This is where most people revert to becoming a "sayer," a term I used earlier. Let's call this person a "talker" instead—someone who talks about the great things they want to accomplish, but for some reason never gets around to it. Maybe they procrastinate, have a fear of failing, or can't manage rejection. They find reasons and excuses not to try or to make the effort to do. Their determination to take that chance on something that might come with risk does not exist.

How do we become a doer? What needs to exist for someone to become a doer of simple tasks and a doer within business, school, job, or team? Is it a mindset? A culture? A list of values?

Well, it's all of these things, and more. It seems so complex and yet mundane. But, rest assured, with a few simple changes in your own daily life, it is really quite simple.

How I Learned to "Do"

I am guilty of this very thing—I've been a talker for years, promising "I'm gonna write a book." Others say the same thing, mostly in jest: "One day, when I write my book . . ." But I never really meant it, until now. I've been talking the talk, too afraid to walk the walk due to a lack of confidence. I mean, I'm a baseball coach, not an author! I usually have a hard time even writing a quality email to my athletic director. I recognize my strengths and weaknesses, and I'm aware that my writing generally needs a bit of polishing.

Now, if you want me to share a story or give a speech, I'm all in! I feel comfortable communicating thoughts, speeches, and ideas orally, in person. I have given hundreds of speeches and rarely write notes. It's not an ego thing; I just speak my mind. I can get my point across better when I talk from my heart than when I read notecards. In fact, the most intimidating thing about writing a book, besides lacking any visual and verbal communication to an audience, is finding ways to share my emotions and passion for leadership and put those thoughts on paper!

How can I get my message across when I would rather be sitting in a classroom, boardroom, or barroom, talking through my thoughts?

When I first started my college coaching career, I wanted to be the best and outwork everyone. I worked to be the best recruiter, the best hitting coach, the best third base coach. I researched and read all the popular coaching books to help me be better at my craft: John Wooden, Lou Holtz, Joe Torre—you name it, I read it. I believed this was going to make me a better coach.

> The culture of an organization is vital for
> long-term success.

But as my career progressed and I navigated through winning and losing seasons, success and failures, I began to look for more than just sports successes. I recognized it was not always about the content—in my case, the baseball lessons—but the culture of the program. The culture of a college baseball team or a business organization is vital for long-term success.

College coaches are often asked to speak at conventions and clinics on topics that revolve around the sport you teach. I always enjoy speaking at these events and have done so multiple times. The crowds mostly consist of high school and youth coaches, trying to pick up ideas and knowledge to run a practice. I like interacting with the crowd and the networking it brings from meeting new and diverse people. I view these speeches as another form of recruiting players; if I can show these high school coaches that I know what I'm talking about, they'll feel comfortable recommending their players to our program.

On one occasion years ago, I was giving a talk on indoor practice plans and how to utilize limitations, such as cold weather in the north, and best maximize your time with players. I finished my talk with a few minutes dedicated to the importance of culture within a team and the value it can bring toward long-term success. I spoke about how you could have all the best ball players, but if they aren't engaged in learning and creating a positive culture, the ultimate goal of winning is difficult.

After my speech, a man approached me and said he loved my content. He explained he was the CEO of a bank and asked if I could come to his business and present my topic to his employees during their upcoming company retreat. I asked him why a bunch of bank tellers and administrators would want to hear me talk about fielding bunt plays in baseball.

He chuckled and explained that he recognized he was having trouble with the culture of his team of employees and loved my ideas revolving around culture. Up until this point in my speaking career, I had never spoken to any group other than baseball coaches, but I accepted his offer and worked to prepare a new PowerPoint presentation.

As I worked on my speech about leadership and culture, I felt that I was actually learning more about the topic I am so passionate about, leadership. I was hooked. I clearly had a "light bulb" moment; I was convinced I had found a new avenue to address with my own team to make them better. I found that I needed to take the time I was spending on the "content" of teaching baseball and invest in the culture of my own organization if I wanted to sustain long-term success.

My leadership speech to the group of bankers was a great success! After a standing ovation, everyone told me they felt energized to tackle their workday. I also felt satisfied. I was happy a group of people could be so engaged in my topic. Giving a speech solely dedicated to leadership was a new one for me at that point of my career, and a bit out of my comfort zone. But afterward, I felt exactly like I do when I give that pump-up locker room speech right before we take the field.

"Now, fellas, let's play our best. Go get 'em! Ready—1, 2, 3, WIN!"

More and more, I began giving speeches and talks to groups about my ideas of success and building a strong culture. I presented ideas that had worked for me in my early days of coaching 18- to 22-year-old Division I athletes. One talk led to another and another and I continued to learn about myself as I prepared for each speech. The preparation process allowed me to learn tactics, study theories, and constantly observe others from whom to pick up leadership traits.

Then I had a stroke of good fortune. A dear friend who is a successful financial advisor recommended that I read a book about giving back to those who are closest to us. Up until that point, most of my reading was about sport successes, written by successful coaches. Basically, the theory of the book my buddy gave to me was that the more you gave, the more you would ultimately receive—a very well thought-out and successful strategy.

I couldn't get enough of this sort of thing: "Leadership 101," "How to Build an Empire," and many more. There are certainly a ton of leadership books out there, and I felt like I read them all.

I would seek out friends, donors, and alums who built successful businesses so I could pick their brains about what made them successful. I reached out to big companies to get in front of CEOs, even for just five minutes, to gather a tidbit of information to file in my storage bank. The information I received allowed my leadership speeches to grow in content. I started to do fewer and fewer sports talks to baseball audiences and more presentations to banks, businesses, car dealerships, HR meetings, roofing companies, police departments, shoe companies, schools, and many more. I would talk to anyone who was interested in having me share my message.

Invest in Relationships

We're all familiar with the concept of turning a negative into a positive, which is easy to "say" but tough to "do."

About the time I was engaged in these leadership talks, I was coaching baseball at the University of Maine, and was given a great opportunity to turn a not-so-great situation into a positive one.

As coaches at UMaine, we not only had to coach, but had to raise funds in order to offset or enhance the programs' operating budgets. If you wanted to turf the field or build a batting cage to improve your facilities, you had to raise the funds. No university funds at all were available for any sort of project. If you wanted to take a spring trip to Florida with your team to beat the long cold days of March, you would need to organize an alumni golf outing for people to donate to offset the costs of that trip. Our program accomplished this by doing little fundraising activities like running a youth camp or starting a club where donors and alums could support the team with annual gifts of $100.

About this time, the university, like most around the country, began to have financial troubles, and most budgets were cut by as much as 25 percent. This would have a huge impact on things like operating budgets and recruiting, which would surely impact the success of these programs. The money needed could not be achieved though small fundraisers, like selling T shirts and running bake sales.

I decided I would take on the role of a fundraiser by meeting some of the generous donors and alums, hoping a few of them could help close the financial gap with larger annual donations. I began to cultivate relationships with a few successful supporters of the school.

Although my goal was to raise funds, I quickly learned that building these relationships was more personally rewarding. These individuals were highly successful in their fields of work, and I quickly realized there was an opportunity to learn just how they became successful. What was the secret sauce to build a multimillion-dollar company?

Surprisingly, all these successful people had similar paths to success. Their stories paralleled one another. Through this monumental task of raising funds to keep our program advancing, I found a great opportunity to learn and to fuel my desire to learn more about positive, successful culture. I initially set out to raise some serious cash to support the baseball program, but I was given so much more. I asked questions and listened to remarkable stories, trying to be a sponge to soak it all up. I quickly recognized these opportunities could be applied to my own team, and could be exactly what I was looking for to be a better coach through my good fortune of being around some of the greatest leaders and builders of culture. After each speech, inevitably someone in the group would ask me where they could find my book. I was stunned. I'm a baseball coach, not an author, I'd tell them.

Most of the time I would pull out a flash drive and download my PowerPoint for them. This became a long process, especially when everyone saw me doing this. I would get letters at my office containing empty flash drives and a note asking me to send them my presentation.

All along, I was still getting asked about writing a book. I can honestly say that writing a book was "out of left field" for me. Yet I set out to turn the negative of having to become a fundraiser into a positive. The great success stories I now possessed helped me become a better mentor and coach to a bunch of college kids. Coupled with ideas to share with businesses and organizations outside the sports world, this was such a positive for me.

Over the years, I have been fortunate to be gifted valuable information on success from strong business leaders and applied that to my sport. Their gains didn't happen by accident. Each one might have had a different footprint, but their paths to success are quite similar.

Nike: "Just Do It"

I finally decided to follow that famous Nike slogan. I told myself that I can be more than just a college baseball coach. Enough with just saying I want to write a book; time to conquer my fear of communicating through writing and *do it*. It was time to stop talking the talk and finally walk the walk.

What transpired from the experiences I gained from success, and more times when I failed, led me to share my ideas, experiences, stories, and thoughts. Ultimately, I came to believe in the power of being a "doer."

> It was time to stop talking the talk and finally walk the walk.

So, if a college baseball coach can write a book about leadership, you certainly can do anything you set out to do! Be persistent, and when you decide to accomplish a task, find a way to get it done. Don't just talk about it—do it.

Remember: never hit that snooze button at 6 a.m. when the list of chores is going through your head. Find the will power to "just do it."

Coach's Challenge

1. Give an example from your job where a particular task or initiative was just talked about, as opposed to acted upon.

2. List three important relationships you currently have that have an impact on your workday.

3. Name three people you can work to build better relationships with at work who can have a positive influence on your role within your organization.

4. What one thing at your workplace and one thing in your personal life can you set out and "just do"? What will it take to make it happen?

19

True Success

I have a small yet powerful exercise I do quite frequently. Whether I am speaking to an organization about leadership or engaging in a one-on-one conversation, I find it fascinating to ask people about their idea of true success. I ask this question to get an immediate response—I want the first thought that comes to mind. Most of the responses go something like this:

"I want to have enough money to retire and take care of my family."

"I hope to be able to send my kids to a great college."

"I want to provide my family with a great place to live and allow us to travel to expand their experiences."

"I would love to be on TV and in the movies."

I look for a quick response because it is usually followed up with what I label a guilty conscience answer:

"But most important is the health of my family, and happiness."

Naturally, we all want our family and ourselves to be healthy and happy. That is really what we are trying to get to when we strive to be successful. But what this means is that most people associate health and happiness, or success, with money, possessions, and fame, which is perfectly okay. Who wouldn't be happy with a stress-free lifestyle because finances were not a concern? But as we outlined earlier, focusing on money as the path to success usually drives a leader down the path of a dictator, for short-lived gains. This is not sustainable when it comes to a strong program or organization.

> Leadership will serve as a guide to long-term success, and always requires attention to your core values.

After conversing about the ideas of success, I take a pause with the people I speak with and demonstrate not only what true success is, but how you and your organization can sustain it for the long term.

Leadership will serve as a guide to long-term success, and always requires attention to your core values, many of which we have previously discussed. Along with investing in ways to create a positive culture, these core values will aid in the quest to reach organizational success.

Once the money, possessions, and fame discussion happens with the people I speak with, I like to break it down in a much different perspective for them. After years of speaking to great leaders in the business and sports worlds, I have found that most have followed a common foundation when they set out to lead their program or organization to success. I have been fortunate to engage in one-on-one discussions with people like Harold Alfond, Senator Susan Collins, Larry and Kevin Mahaney, Charles Johnson (founder of Franklin Templeton Investments), and John Mullen (the volunteer coach who wanted to give back). These are just a few of the people who gave to their communities, developed ground-breaking products, and built companies from the ground up. It wasn't luck or an inheritance that made it happen; they weren't given a "silver spoon," or a handbook that outlined what to do. Yet each one carved a similar path to becoming successful.

When it comes to sustained, true success, four key steps need to happen. If there is one message I wish to send throughout this book, it is these four steps of true success. Up until now, we discussed values, traits, and culture builders that help create a positive and strong environment within an organization. Coupled with our core values, these four steps are what you need to strive for to gain success for your organization, team, or company.

1. Surround Yourself with Good People, and Good Things Happen

The first thing that has to happen is you have to have the confidence as a leader to find good people to surround yourself with. This can be challenging, because the hiring/recruiting process is something that we learn from experience.

Ask yourself, "What is a good person?" and "What are my values?"

List the values and traits that are important to and your organization. Look back at the values wall: positive attitude, image, real energy, integrity, commitment, toughness, and so on.

When searching for these quality people, think about whether they possess a strong foundation you want to mentor and grow with? Do they have an optimistic attitude? Is it contagious? Are they willing to grow? Do they have the ability to be a winner as we just outlined a few chapters ago? Do they value their image and that of the organization? Can they communicate? Do they have real energy and work ethic?

The process of finding your team members is both critical and essential. Surrounding yourself with people you can both work and grow with will allow you to be much more productive yourself.

Of course, there are factors affecting who you can hire. One is salary pool. The higher the salary offered, the larger the applicant pool. Yet some of the greatest hires and recruits don't necessarily have the most years of experience or command the highest salaries. Some applicants simply possess a foundation to grow, especially when properly mentored. Sometimes you have to look beyond the polished resume to find what might be a diamond in the rough.

I look at it this way when searching for recruits and people to join our program. I want to find applicants who demonstrate they have a few of the core values I believe in. Then it is up to me, as the leader, to grow, mold, and mentor them. Some of the best people I have been fortunate to have join our program have been first-year, start-up volunteer coaches.

> Find someone who demonstrates they
> have a few of the core values you
> believe in.

Talk about grinders – they are people willing to work full-time hours, for free! They look for an experience you can provide them to help them grow, and their form of compensation is *you*! This is a huge responsibility: they are willing to do the job in return for what you can provide in the form of leadership and development. This step is critical when finding the people you believe have the traits you require.

2. Relationships: Work at It

The next step in obtaining true success is by far the most time consuming. Once the team is in place, strong relationships have to be fostered with each member. It takes large amounts of personal time, energy, and even money to invest in them. But the returns pay huge dividends. Your skills as a communicator, mentor, and teacher will certainly be put to the test. But your employees will see your dedication to them and the relationship you are fostering, which leads them to believe you are truly invested in them. You don't treat them as a pawn in a game; you care about their thoughts, well-being, and professional development.

> Your employees will see your dedication to them and the relationship you are fostering.

Be prepared to navigate ways to invest the time necessary. This is why I mentioned that building relationships can be the hardest step. Not every leader is willing to invest the personal time in their people, their team. They "talk the talk" of building relationships, but are they willing to "walk the walk"? It can take away from other responsibilities you have within the organization. It is even more critical when you first start at your business or new role as a leader. This is when all eyes are on you. Are you a dictator or a server? Do you empower your people?

It might mean you have to take time to visit someone outside the office. Set up a dinner on a weekend. Invite someone into your home. Attend one of your employees' kids' Little League games, even if it means missing your own son's or daughter's events.

I mentioned earlier that I became the head baseball coach at Stetson University in the winter of 2016. Most coaches are hired at the end of the college baseball season, which is typically in the months of June and July. So it was quite out of the ordinary to be named a Division I coach in the middle of the school year, only three weeks from opening day of the season. Looking back on it, how was I really supposed to know the players I was about to coach? I only had a few weeks to learn about them before we embarked on playing games. In fact, that first month, I was focused on making sure I knew all their names, let alone being able to teach them my systems, baseball signs, and philosophy.

As the 2017 season began, we pretty much stunk up the place. We were not good, plain and simple. But I sensed the players were willing to work hard, listen, and be very open to new things. I knew right then I had to focus as much as I could on building better relationships with each one of them. I took the time to ask them about themselves. Where were they from? What were their favorite movies? And, of course, we focused on being better each day, both on the playing field and with our relationships.

About halfway through the regular season, the team started playing better. This team had been picked in the preseason poll to finish in seventh place in the ASUN conference. Yet as conference play began, the team started to gel. They played better each day, and finished the season in a respectable second place.

My relationships with the players returning for the 2018 season was still in its infancy, being only four months old. So I decided to invest as much time as possible to build on them. In most summer months, college baseball players leave their teams and head out to one of the many college summer leagues around the country. Whether it is the Alaskan league, the Cape Cod league in Massachusetts, the West Coast league in Oregon, the Coastal Plains league in the Carolinas, or the Northwoods league through the Midwest, players join these teams for approximately eight weeks to get more playing experience. This helps the college players be better prepared once they return to their college team the next season. So it is common practice to have players from a college team scattered throughout the country during the summer months in one of these leagues.

I had a good idea that the returning players for the 2018 team, along with the new additions we were able to recruit in my first four months, had a lot of talent. Yet, I recognized if we wanted to be better in 2018, to be a champion, to reach *success*, I needed to invest in the team's culture. And what better way to start by working on my relationships with each one of them.

What I decided to do that first summer as the Stetson baseball coach was to take a break from the summer recruiting of future players, and travel to as many of our returning players as I could. Most of the time I did this unannounced. I would show up at games of our players in Maryland, Virginia, and Cape Cod. After the game, I would take them out to dinner for a good meal (they usually get sick of pizza and fast food). I wanted to show each returning player I cared about them. I wanted to invest in our relationships.

Earlier I mentioned the success of the 2018 Stetson baseball team, winning 48 games and finishing with a ranking of fourth in the country. Although I would love to take credit for aiding in the most successful season in Stetson Baseball history because I drove halfway around the country visiting with our guys, I can't do that. I think it happened because we had five pitchers throwing the ball in the mid-nineties and a group of tough, talented young men, but maybe it helped us to a successful season by building those relationships.

To be invested in your people, you have to work on these critical relationships every day. You may have great people, but it is essential to build those relationships to navigate through the success process. Keep in mind that each relationship is different and there is no timetable to establish them. That can be the tricky part—one employee might feel a strong connection to you in a relatively short time, while another will take time to grow. But when you build them well, the team is ready to do great work together.

3. Trust

After you feel you have a strong connection to your people from the time and effort you've invested, the next step starts to take shape. This is when you truly get to know your people and they learn about you.

The strong bond you build helps everyone in the organization to build trust within themselves—trust in the core values, in the vision of the company, and in you, as their leader! The trust you have from your people allows them to work at a higher level. The "shoulda, woulda, coulda" person we spoke about in Chapter 17 will become nonexistent. The team moves in one direction, which is the direction you, as the leader, deems the right way. Great focus on the tasks at hand takes place daily and in a consistent pattern. Program and organizational goals are not only established, but begin to be obtained. Each person senses a clear path because each one knows their role within the organization. The presence of trust in the people you surround yourself with opens up many doors for you to mentor and teach your team. You can be yourself.

> The strong bond you build helps everyone in the organization to build trust within themselves.

What I mean by being yourself within the organization is that most people feel limited in their own organization because of restrictions. You feel like your hands are tied, whether due to a policy or rule, or maybe because the leader is afraid of offending someone, afraid to fail.

A big part of being a leader is that you don't necessarily need to build friendships with the people you are leading, but you need to have their respect in order to lead them. Having trust among you and your team members allows you to lead in the way *you* feel comfortable, not what is comfortable for others.

I made this mistake when I was just starting out as a young college coach. My college coach, Coach Holowaty, was someone whom I not only looked up to, but idolized. He was tough, demanding, and pushed me and my teammates to limits I never imagined I had. He probably was too tough on most, and some jumped ship. Yet I connected with his style. I truly believe I would not be even close to the coach, father, husband, and co-worker I am today if it was not for his influences. He taught me not to be afraid to fail. He guided me to appreciate the core principles and values I continue to invest in each day.

The mistake I made in my first years as a coach was that I tried to be Coach Holowaty – in every way! It worked for him, and I believed in the ways he approached coaching and life. I thought the path to success was to mimic him. I used the same phrases, and I even tried to walk like him. Not until a few years later did I finally figure out that I had to be me. I certainly could use what he taught me, but I needed to mold it into how I teach, share, and communicate.

Early in my career, my players saw right though me, resulting in them not fully trusting me. It's difficult to trust someone or something where you don't have a connection or feel it's genuine. They were respectful and dedicated, and to this day I still have great relationships with many of them. But I didn't give them my best. Not because I wasn't trying, but because I wasn't ready or able to. Learning how to be yourself allows you to become a better teacher, mentor, and leader.

Trust does not give you a free pass to go outside the core values and the rules that are established within your organization. Rather, the trust you build allows you to work with your counterparts and employees in a safe, fun, productive, positive, and competitive environment.

4. Loyalty, the Final Path to Success

As a leader, you've found some really good people for your team. You chose them. You invested tons of time by building relationships with your people, which enabled trust to form, which allows everyone to believe in the process you set forth, as their leader.

The final step is about to be complete, which is loyalty. This means your team believes in you and the environment you created for them. They thank you every day for that with their loyalty. If someone speaks ill of you or your organization, your team defends you and has your back. They protect the "house," or the program. They will stay late to finish the project, or work weekends to get the job done. "Whatever it takes, boss, let's get it done!"

By the way, this can be awfully contagious! The loyalty your employees demonstrate is the reason your group becomes more and more successful. I find that most people, including great leaders, are pleasers—they want others to acknowledge them with signs of gratitude when they accomplish a task. It can be a form of fuel that drives a person.

> When you create an environment that can foster loyalty, you will see production rise.

So when loyalty exists within your organization, you basically have people who want to please one another and their leader. This is present all the time with most successful businesses. Are the employees working late because they have to or because they want to? Are employees loyal enough to sustain the image of your company and willing to pick up the empty coffee cup from the lobby floor of your office building and put it in the trash? Are you willing to replace the paper towels in the restroom?

Or do you think it's "not in my job description," that it is beneath you to do such a small, mundane task? When you create an environment that can foster loyalty, you will see production rise.

True Success Isn't About Money, Possessions, or Fame

Most people believe success is measured by how much money, possessions, or fame you have. However, if you can see the true value in gathering great people for your team, this leads to a great start in the success process. Next, invest a lot of time and energy in building relationships with them. Trust and loyalty are sure to develop, and can help long-term success grow within your organization or team. Members of your organization are happy, productive, and hard working. They like to compete and look to make a great effort each day. They become contagious. They grow more and more positive each day. The production of your team goes up, beating the competition to accounts, leading to new business.

Guess what happens when these four steps occur and long-term success develops? In the business world, CEOs report growth and better earnings. Stock prices go up. Employees are awarded bonuses and raises for their part in growing the business. Those same employees most likely run to the local dealers to buy boats and cars and take nice vacations with their family. And the CEOs get a chance to do interviews and articles on why their company is rapidly growing toward becoming a Fortune 500 company. So, in the end, everyone receives the money, possessions, and fame they originally sought. In sports, it's wins and championships. Yet the money, possessions, fame, and wins are not measures of success. They are rewards from investing in a set of core values, building a strong culture, and working hard to establish a positive environment to be successful.

Building these relationships of trust, loyalty, and work ethic with the people you choose to surround yourself with in your organization are absolutely vital to long-term success. If you, as a leader, have a truly genuine and honest approach to caring for the people of your company or team, your path to a successful culture will start to take shape. However, if you choose not to invest in these four key principles, it's going to be an uphill battle. And please understand, this is a *process*. It will take time and much effort on your part to invest in the four steps to success.

The Puzzle Changes

Let's say after all the time, energy, and even sometimes the money you personally invest in these four principles, you see positive results. People are excited to work for you, production is soaring, and you love to have meetings with your team to celebrate the success. You believe you figured out the puzzle that leads to the pathway for success. Now it's time to kick back, smell those roses, and enjoy it. There certainly is value in celebrating your team's accomplishments.

> Just because you think you figured out
> the secret sauce of success one year does
> not mean it will work again.

However, as time goes by, the challenges your organization faces inevitably will change. Employees will move on to other jobs, and accounts will come and go. These puzzle pieces—the people, products, technology, and so on —are on the move. Just because you think you figured out the secret sauce of success one year does not mean it will work again. As a leader, you need to recognize your puzzle pieces and how they all fit together.

We see this all the time in sports. A certain team can do no wrong one year, completely dominating the league with a talented group, leading to a championship. Then the next season, that same team can't get out of the cellar in the standings, even with the same roster.

Many factors are out of your control, such as injuries, change in leadership, employees, and overall culture shifts that can lead to a change in production. It could also be equated to having a laissez-faire attitude. Ever heard of the fat cat syndrome? That's when you get so successful that you become complacent and sit around like a lazy fat cat, content with letting opportunities pass you by. It feels like yesterday, hearing Coach Holowaty scream to the team at our practice after a ten-game winning streak, "Don't be fat cats! Let's get to work!"

My point is, culture is ever changing. It *cannot* be neglected, not for a second. If you let your guard down as a leader, or take some time off from investing in culture, that's when it slips. Everyone goes through ups and downs, wins and losses. Yet when I look at companies, teams, people, and organizations that have stood the test of time as they successfully navigated though the muck and continually invested in their culture, those are the ones that figured out the ever-changing puzzle that leads to true success.

Coach's Challenge

1. How do you define true success?

2. List those who have taught you about loyalty, trust, leadership, and success.

3. What are some positive and effective ways you have invested in the relationships in your work and personal life?

4. How do you demonstrate loyalty within your team or organization?

Afterword

On Monday, December 19, 2016, Stetson University announced the appointment of Steve Trimper as head coach of men's baseball, following the outstanding career of Hall of Fame Coach Pete Dunn. During the search for a new coach, Jeff Altier, director of athletics and Stetson alumnus, had described Steve to me as the "whole package." Indeed, he told me that Steve was more than simply a coach, but rather that he was a remarkable leader. Full of energy, full of charisma, full of positivity. An eager student of success and a passionate communicator.

Now that you have read Steve's book, you understand what we all saw in Steve, and the reason he is able to catalyze members of our Hatter baseball team to give their all for the game. Moreover, his enthusiasm drives members of the university community and those who live in our area to come out and watch the Stetson Hatters play America's pastime in the hot Florida sun.

But, as you have probably noted, this book isn't about Steve Trimper or his baseball coaching skills. You don't have to be an NCAA Division I coach to learn from Steve's message about leadership. What I love the most in his message is how little things count along with the big ones. Small interactions with everyday people, moments like the one in the airport restaurant where attitude made or broke the encounter—and led Steve to

225

learn the lessons that came from those interactions. And Steve is a better leader because of them.

So, how does this relate to the way you will move forward to develop your personal brand of leadership? Certainly, the Coach's Challenge questions at the end of each chapter give you ample opportunity to look at your own leadership style and consider how to enhance your performance and success.

But I encourage you to "go beyond" (as we would say at Stetson) and start looking for the lessons you can learn from the special interactions you have with people whom you know well or do not know at all. Did you get a strong and warm handshake or encounter the connection from locking eyes with someone when the two of you met? Did you feel drawn to someone's positive outlook on life or commitment to taking the high road in a difficult situation? Did you sense the special magnetism of a keynote speaker at a luncheon or the quiet confidence of a veteran coach or school teacher?

All of these people are leaders and we can learn to model ourselves after them as Steve has done. Some leaders may be born, but this book reminds us that many leaders are made. You can choose every morning to be a "grinder"; you can choose to keep your eyes on the future but remember the details; you can choose to keep a strong ego and hear the praise, but give the credit to everyone who had a hand in lifting you up. Great leaders choose their futures and take their cues from those they will lead. They are continually learning from one another and fashioning their learning to make a difference.

I encourage you to keep Steve's book on your shelf and check it often: when you have a hugely successful day or have just crashed and burned; when you meet your expectations for yourself or when you miss the mark entirely. Take a lesson from

Steve and write down the encounters that made an impression on you and talk with others about them. Keep an open mind and keep communicating.

We are all able to develop into great leaders by learning from those who inspire us. Let this book sit high on your inspiring list and move ahead with passion and confidence.

Wendy B. Libby, Ph.D.
president, Stetson University
DeLand, Florida
September 2019

Acknowledgments

For much of my life, writing a book was the furthest thing from my mind. But so many times I found myself joking about comical and/or interesting situations that happened to me throughout my career that I thought to myself, if I ever write a book, I'm going to include this story. Lo and behold, with the encouragement of many close friends and colleagues, I decided to take a leap of faith, and here I sit, writing my first book.

Recording my personal ideas and experiences on paper has been both difficult and exhilarating, especially as a rookie. Fortunately, many people in my life have had a profound impact on my career and have contributed to my professional journey. They have been by my side, allowing me to grow, fail, and flourish.

This book would not have been possible without the help of three tremendous leaders in my life. Bob Byrnes, former athletic director at Manhattan College, gave me my first opportunity to be a Division I Head Coach Baseball Coach at a very young age. He taught me how to be tough and resilient. His ability to push me to my limits drove me to learn and thrive in the college baseball profession.

Next, Blake James, athletic director at the University of Miami, believed in me and gave me the opportunity at UMaine to take a step up in the coaching ranks. He taught me how to connect with people. His ability to form relationships and genuinely care for people, no matter how high or low on the totem pole, is something I would never have learned without his leadership.

Third, Jeff Altier gave me the chance to lead a top-level program. I was a complete outsider, in last place on the candidate list prior to the interview process at Stetson. He showed faith in me and took a calculated risk, hiring a fast-talking guy from the north. Jeff gave me the gift of optimism, as he sees the good in every situation, no matter how bleak.

Stacy Turner really runs the department at Stetson (that's a joke, Jeff!), and I can't begin to thank her enough for all she has done for my career, and for loyalty and friendship with my family. She is a true Energizer Bunny, and I make a point to be around her for a small part of my day so I can catch some of her contagious positive attitude.

I am eternally grateful to my college coach, Bill Holowaty. Coach was the first person in my life to build leadership within me. He was there for me on the field of play, but his best gift was how much he was there for me in my life—and continues to be. If you're fortunate enough to label someone your father figure, you've got it pretty good. Coach is that and then some for me.

A very special thanks to Stetson president Dr. Wendy Libby for her unwavering leadership of one of the most beautiful universities in the country and her loyalty to the Stetson community. And to her husband, Richard, for his companionship, stories, and guidance when I needed a shoulder to cry on.

To Tom Savage, Dennis Libbey, Ann Maxim, and Stuart Price, who talked me off the ledge on many cold dark days with their ultimate positivity and support. They supported my career in many ways, and are true friends long after my days at UMaine were done.

To Kevin Mahaney, who followed in the footsteps of his father and showed me how to drive for success. He is an inspiring person, who taught me that if you want to reach a goal, the only thing holding you back is yourself.

Writing this book has been a humbling and surreal process. I want to thank the folks at Wiley, particularly Jeanenne Ray, for taking a chance on a baseball coach to write a book, and Peter Knox and Victoria Anllo, for bringing me to Wiley in Hoboken, New Jersey, and opening my eyes to the professionalism they bring to their company. Last but certainly not least, thank you to Vicki Adang, my editor. I can envision her rolling her eyes the day she found out she had to work with a first-time writer and college coach. Her humor, professionalism, and knowledge built my confidence, something I never believed existed. She has motivated me in the same circle as the great people in my life.

To best-selling author Jon Gordon, who returned my email four years ago, ten minutes after I wrote to him and gave me the advice just to write. Don't worry about how to spell, go out and tell your story, he said.

Coaching for more than 27 years has brought me in touch with so many great young athletes. They truly have been the ones who allowed me to test my leadership skills and helped me grow when I screwed it up. Of all the people in my professional life, the ones I cherish the most are the student athletes I was fortunate to coach. They don't realize how much they coached me as well.

To the 2018 Stetson Hatters baseball team: thank you for trusting me and believing we had the ability to make a run deep in the season and strive for Omaha. You all set the foundation at this university for greatness in the coming years.

A head coach is only as good as the assistants around them. Coaching can be a very egotistical business, yet there are some people who not only help me, but also taught me things I could not have taught myself. Dave Therneau, Joe Mercadante,

Brandon Brewer, Mark Michaud, and Tyler Packanick all bring a unique personality to complete our staff in such a fun and positive way. I want to thank Mike Cole, Kevin Leighton, Jared Holowaty, Billy Cather, and Nick Derba, all of whom have moved on to become college head coaches, for their dedication. Ryan Forrest, John Schiffner, Tom Sowinski, John Mullen, and Mike Mora were by my side many days building our programs.

To all the support staff in my career who put up with my "bull in a china shop" approach—Alicia Queally, Mike McKercher, Ricky Hazel, Mark Wateska, Elise Paulson, John Travnick, Brad Keith, Rick Hall, Linda Thayer, Steve Jones, Debbie Gregory, Pat McBride, Bill Currier, Jeff Schulman, Dr. Dave Worthley...many thanks. Ed Hockenbury—thank you for teaching me how to use the phrase "in conjunction with."

I value the many friends and family who helped me decompress from my job, or give me a pick-me-up talk and kept me going: Chief Jason Umberger, Bob Cutler, Tiger Stewart, Keven Ireland, Scott Murray, Charles and Mary Budd, Joe Ferris, John Reed, Rob Carmichael, Daren Seekins, Major General Douglas Farnham, Paul Benzing, Jim and Jamie Schneider, Joe Cushman, Russ Goff, Neil Trimper, and Glen Trimper. Appreciation also goes to Charles Johnson for inspiring me to finish this project.

To Mike Bozzuto, and Megan and Eric Weinberger, thanks for showing me the value of giving, and how the more you give, the more you get in return.

Finally, anyone in the sports world can speak to the number of hours it can take away from family. Travel, recruiting trips, donor visits, and late-night calls from players in need of encouragement all add up to missed time with loved ones.

Everyone occasionally has work-related issues that get put before family in order to balance job and life. But for college or professional sports coaches, there is something to say for the real coaches in this profession and our lives: the coach's spouse.

My career, this book, and any success I have had up to this point in my life wouldn't have happened without my wife, Lisa. She holds the titles of psychologist, motivational coach, team mom, cook, recruiting coordinator, book editor, sounding board, chauffeur to airports at 4 a.m., donor relations specialist, contract negotiator, family lawyer and accountant, and medical insurance specialist to name just a few. She also listens to my rants after a bad practice or game, always to tell a joke or give me a tip on how tomorrow will be better. And all of this is along with her other roles as full-time mom and wellness coordinator.

Lisa's dedication, along with that of my twin daughters, Ally and Morgan, have made my success possible. Every family vacation as the twins were growing up involved at least three to five baseball games to see a recruit, or a stop on the way to a water park to visit a turf field that I wanted to see. I can't get back all the youth hockey games and high school graduations I missed because of a baseball game, but I was able to be successful because of your love. I am so proud of all three of you. I preach "Surround yourself with good people and good things will happen." Well, I surrounded myself with three loving, smart, and talented ladies.

Love you guys. SLAM 4

About the Author

A veteran of more than 20 years as a Division I college baseball head coach, **Steve Trimper** has seen it all during his career. From having to sod a field in New York City to give his team a place to practice and play while coaching at Manhattan, to leading the Stetson Hatters onto the field rated as one of the best in the nation in 2018, Trimper has always been about doing the work to help his student-athletes become the best they can be.

A Coach of the Year selection in three different NCAA Division 1 conferences, Trimper led his Manhattan team for seven seasons, setting a program record for single-season victories. He took over a historically successful program in Maine in 2006, guiding the Black Bears to three America East titles and two berths in the NCAA Tournament.

In 2017, Trimper took over the Stetson baseball program and in just his second season, led the Hatters to their best season in program history. The 2018 Stetson team set a school record, with 18 consecutive victories on the way to tying the program mark with 48 wins and a top 10 final national ranking. The Hatters hosted an NCAA Regional in DeLand for the first time, winning and advancing to the first NCAA Super Regional in school history.

In addition to his coaching career, Trimper is a highly sought motivational speaker who is equally at home addressing coaches and corporate executives. He and his wife, Lisa, have twin daughters, Ally and Morgan, who are members of the women's hockey team at the University of Maine.

Index